Tell Me Another Story

Tell Me Another Story

More Stories from the Waldorf Early Childhood Association of North America

Edited by Louise deForest
Illustrations by Deborah Grieder and Jo Valens

WECAN
WALDORF EARLY CHILDHOOD
ASSOCIATION OF NORTH AMERICA

Tell Me Another Story: More Stories from the Waldorf Early Childhood Association of North America
First English Edition
© 2019 Waldorf Early Childhood Association of North America
ISBN: 978-1-936849-50-5

Editor: Louise deForest
Cover Design: Deborah Grieder and Lory Widmer
Illustrations: Deborah Grieder and Jo Valens
Copy editing and graphic design: Lory Widmer
We are grateful to all who contributed stories to this collection.
Please see page 239 for information about the stories and their tellers.

This publication was made possible by a grant
from the Waldorf Curriculum Fund.

Waldorf Early Childhood Association of North America
285 Hungry Hollow Rd.
Spring Valley, NY 10977
845-352-1690
info@waldorfearlychildhood.org
www.waldorfearlychildhood.org

For a complete book catalog, contact WECAN or visit our online store:
store.waldorfearlychildhood.org

Contents

STORIES FOR WINTER TIME

STORIES FOR TIMES IN NEED OF SPECIAL CARE

STORIES FOR ANYTIME

Introduction

LOUISE deFOREST

MANY YEARS AGO, my almost middle-aged son, going through a major life event, asked me to tell him the story he so loved when he was four years old. That story was *The Three Billy Goats Gruff*, a story of an ominous encounter, of family, and of overcoming obstacles in one's path. When he was four, he asked to hear that story every night for months, and, while I found the repetition tedious it was obvious that for him it was important. At five years old, an event occurred in his life that he struggled with well into his adult years, and it was then that I understood why he needed to hear that one story so many times. That particular story brought to him a picture of the future—of *his* future—and at the same time gave him tools with which to overcome the obstacle, as well as the self-confidence to feel that it was, indeed, possible. Hearing that little story over and over again strengthened him for what lay ahead and awakened the courage he would need to move forward and overcome his "troll." For him, and I dare say for us all, stories act as the far-off light shining in the darkness of the night.

And that is the beauty of stories, be they fairy tales, legends, nature stories, or stories taken from your own life. All stories are *our* stories; all stories offer guidance, support, and a context within which we may understand the events in our own lives. And if nothing else, stories offer each one of us relief—a moment when we can escape our everyday realities, our complicated lives, and just be a man or a woman or a child, subject to the human traits that rule us all. When we hear or read a story, we are there, sitting at the feet of the storyteller or walking along the stream, leaving behind our daily lives and breathing into the story itself.

There's a Lakota saying that if the storyteller is really good, he or she will let you live through the storm. This is the charm of stories; they transport us out of ourselves long enough so that we can glimpse life more objectively and sympathetically. Then we may perceive that there is rightfulness in consequences and goodness all around us, if only we would stop long enough to see it.

Stories come from a far-off place and exist between here and there: "Once upon a time." In a world where time is of the essence and where everyone, it seems, is under the illusion of not having time, stories can lift us entirely out of time to that wonderful space between waking, dreaming, and sleeping. *Once upon a time* is a definite point in the infinite; it exists somewhere, but where? When? It has no particular date, nor does it need one. In hearing a story, any story, time can stretch from the moment of creation up to that moment which can best be described as *now*. However, these stories, timeless as they are, take place in a world we recognize as the real world, no matter how exotic and strange it may appear to be. They are full of all that is familiar to us, giving us the peace that is so necessary for survival itself.

In our world of too much information, a world of too little heart and too much logic and reason, stories reconnect us to the wonder and the possibilities we knew existed when we were children. Life becomes pregnant with the unexpected, with laughter and genuine tears, and we can feel that anything is possible. We experience once again what all children know; sparks of living glory are in all things—the rocks, the trees, the grasses of the field, and in the human being, as well. As Sherman Apt Russell wrote, "A sense of wonder is not only our starting point. It can also be our sense of direction." A good story is wise in the understanding of human nature and candid in the treatment of it. Indeed, stories are far older than reading and writing and are themselves more like wildflowers in a meadow. They are living, breathing beings, changing imperceptibly as people pass among them, each teller adding her words or rhythms and speaking with the voice of her people.

As Albert Einstein once said, "Logic will get you from A to B. Imagination will get you anywhere." It is obvious today that the forms, attitudes, and consciousness of the past will no longer serve humanity in the future. Children today are pushing us to rethink what we know, to let go of everything that divides us one from another and to look beyond the surface of things to find the inner reality. Collaboration, thinking outside of any box, and an awareness of the connectedness of all things—our mutual dependency—will mark the thinking of the future, and will enable us to meet the challenges of the future. In the stories contained in this book you will find examples of this future consciousness, where all of nature helps those in need; where through inner strength and outer guidance we can face our foes and fears with true uprightness; where through our trials and tribulations we uncover the spirit within us and can live with purpose and nobility.

Today, our all-embracing modern forms of communication threaten the storyteller and, as one storyteller predicted, may end up making us all mute. Ready-made images and entertainment at the push of a button have robbed us and our children of the inner, self-made pictures that are each person's birthright. Those of us who work with young children know how difficult it is to tell them a story these days: what a hard time they have sitting still with all the images in their heads that they don't quite know what to do with. It is hard for them to listen, as well, having shut out the unintelligible and often confusing world of the adults around them. In our times it is increasingly urgent to provide children with images that will feed their souls, images that shine with beauty and, most importantly, truth. Every child (and many of us adults, too) longs to be enveloped in Mother Earth's blanket, warm and cozy, as in the story of the Seed Babies, and all of us can use an apple walk alongside "Grampsy," especially when life has been challenging. Stories can fill our souls with satisfaction and warmth, making us thankful for that foolish, difficult, frail, tender, and noble experience of being a human being on earth.

It is human nature to want to share what we love. Sharing often deepens the pleasure, making the adventures more exciting or the jokes funnier. The stories in this collection have been gathered from Waldorf early childhood teachers all over the country who long to share what they love with those who love children. Many are original tales, created out of the imagination of the teacher; some spring from nature or a seasonal festival, like the seasonal tales you will find here. And some are classic favorites, changed over the years through the telling but still holding all the elements we remember. And, because it is in the sharing—the telling—that a story comes alive, so that we can meet one another in a world outside of time and space, the more you tell stories, the more you will hear, "*Tell me another story.*"

Stories for Spring and Summer Time

Little Spring Bunny

MEG FISHER

Sing "Lippity Lop" or any appropriate springtime "bunny" tune. Then speak the verses:

Little Spring Bunny went out for a walk
To see what he could see.
He sniffed at a flower,
He nibbled some grass,
And he looked up at a tree.

Little Spring Bunny hopped on a log.
He hopped from end to end.
Little Spring Bunny met a frog
And Frog became his friend.

"Oh! What's that?" the bunny cried,
"That's falling from the sky?"
"It's rain! It's rain!" the Froggie said.
"Come in here and keep dry."

Little Spring Bunny and Frog go inside the hollow log.

The sky grew dark,
The wind blew hard.
It was a fierce spring storm.
But all the while inside the log
The friends were dry and warm.

And then at last the sun came out.
The two friends played all day
Until it was their supper time,
And then, they hopped away.

Sing "Song of the Bunnies" or other "bunny" tune.

RESOURCES

Mary Thienes Schünemann, "Lippity Lop" in Sing a Song of Seasons *(Fairfax, California: Naturally You Can Sing 2005), p. 107.*

Marlys Swinger and Margaret Wise Brown, "Song of the Bunnies," in Sing a Song of Seasons, *ibid. p. 45.*

Little Boy Blue

JOANI LACKIE-CALLIGHAN

A puppet play based on the traditional nursery rhyme, inspired by a workshop with Suzanne Down. Except for the main traditional rhyme, which can be sung to the tune with which most teachers are familiar, the little songs in this story are Joani's original words. She performs them accompanied by pentatonic tones and encourages storytellers to make up their own tunes.

IT WAS A BEAUTIFUL SPRING MORNING. Grandpa Blue came out into the farmyard and said good morning to his milk cow and his woolly sheep.

"Good morning, Moo Cow. Good morning, sheep. Today is the day you get your haircut."

Just then, Little Boy Blue came out of the house and began his morning chores.

"I'll help you with the feeding of the animals today, Grandpa!" he said.

Little Boy Blue went to the haystack and brought some hay to the cow. "Now let me milk you, Moo Cow," he said. He sang:

> *"Helping, helping all the day,*
> *Helping in my special way."*

Then Little Boy Blue went and fed the sheep. He sang:

> *"Helping, helping all the day,*
> *Helping in my special way."*

"Thank you, Little Boy Blue," Grandpa Blue said. "This year I will give you a brand-new chore. I am getting old and cannot do the sheep shearing by myself. I will need you to watch over the sheep, and when I give you the word, bring me one sheep for its haircut."

"Oh, no, Grandpa," said Little Boy Blue. "I am still too little. What if the sheep run away from me . . .or try to bite me? No, this I cannot do. Please, just let me feed the animals their food and milk the cow, like always."

"Dear Boy Blue," Grandpa Blue answered lovingly. "You are getting older and I need your help. My legs and arms are not so strong anymore. You have strong muscles and can lead the sheep to the barn. Will you at least try?"

Little Boy Blue's eyes filled with tears, but he took a big breath.

Grandpa sensed his grandson's concern and said, "I forgot to tell you the best part! While I was cleaning the attic, I found my old bugle horn. I will give it to you, and if you find yourself needing a little help with the sheep, just give a toot on the horn and I will come running."

Grandpa Blue handed Little Boy Blue the bugle and asked Little Boy Blue to bring the first sheep to the barn.

Little Boy Blue set the horn down by the haystack and went to the sheep pen. He opened the pen and picked up the first sheep to take to Grandpa Blue. He never thought about closing the pen behind him.

Little Boy Blue came out of the barn, not realizing how tired he had become. He sat down beside the haystack and closed his eyes.

He did not notice when the cow walked right past him and went into the cornfield.

He did not notice when the sheep walked right past him to go and nibble the fresh grass and clover in the meadow.

He did not notice, because Little Boy Blue was fast asleep.

At noon, Grandma Blue came out with her picnic basket filled with lunch for Grandpa and Little Boy Blue.

She saw the cow in the cornfield, the sheep in the meadow, and Little Boy Blue asleep.

She went to the barn yelling, "Old Man, come quick!"

When Grandpa came out of the barn and saw the empty pen, he called out: "Little Boy Blue, come blow your horn. The sheep's in the meadow, the cow's in the corn."

He looked at Grandma and asked: "Where is the little boy who looks after the sheep?"

She answered: "He's under the haystack fast asleep. Will you wake him?"

Grandpa answered: "No, not I. For if I do, he's sure to cry."

"Leave it to me," Grandma replied. And she went to the haystack and gently woke up Little Boy Blue with a little tickle and a song:

> *"Waking, waking on this day,*
> *In my special Grandma way."*

Little Boy Blue woke with a start and looked around.

When he saw the pen empty he was about to grab his horn, but instead he looked at Grandma and said, "I will get them to the pen right away."

As soon as Little Boy Blue picked up the first sheep, the rest followed him to the pen.

Grandma Blue looked at Grandpa Blue and said, "I think we will have to start calling him Big Boy Blue from now on."

And that is just what they did.

Sing "Little Boy Blue":

> *Little Boy Blue, come blow your horn,*
> *The sheep's in the meadow, the cow's in the corn.*
> *Where is the little boy who looks after the sheep?*
> *He's under the haystack, fast asleep.*
> *Will you wake him? No, not I,*
> *For if I do he's sure to cry.*

RESOURCES

"Little Boy Blue," traditional nursery song. In Mary Thienes Schünemann, Lavender's Blue Dilly-Dilly *(Fairfax, California: Naturally You Can Sing 2004), p. 19.*

A Legend of the Pussywillows

A POLISH FABLE ADAPTED BY DIANE VAN DOMMELEN

THE SUN WAS BRAVELY SHINING in a blue sky. It was so early in the spring that snow still covered the meadow, though it was beginning to soften and melt into muddy puddles. And the newly ice-free brook was bubbling quite merrily in its bed.

At the far side of the meadow, in the cozy barn, Mother Cat was tending her kittens. The kittens were fluffy and grey, and they were very frisky!

On an especially warm and sunny afternoon, mother cat led her kittens out of the barn and to the edge of the meadow. They were so excited and ran here and there, looking at everything! Mother Cat tried very hard to keep them close by, but just then the first spring butterflies flittered and fluttered over the heads of the kittens. The kittens chased those butterflies right across the meadow and to the banks of the brook.

Splish! Splash! Right into the brook they fell!

"Mew! Mew!" they cried. "Help us! Help us! We do not like water! We cannot swim! Mew! Mew!"

Mother Cat followed the cries of her babies and saw the kittens struggling in the bubbling water of the brook.

"Meow!" she cried. "Who will save my kittens?"

Only the willows growing on the banks of the brook heard the cries of Mother Cat and her kittens and saw the kittens bobbing up and down.

Leaning over the water as far as they could, they said to the kittens, "Grab hold of us with your sharp little claws. We will lift you to safety."

The kittens reached up towards the willows and caught hold with their claws. The willows rose slowly back up with the kittens holding on tightly. When they were over land again, the willows held still, while the kittens climbed down and ran to their mother, who cuddled them warm and dry.

Now, up in the blue sky, the Sun had seen everything, and he blessed the kind willows. Since that day, when the spring sun begins to shine and the snows begin to melt, the willows grow soft, grey buds that look just like the paws of the little pussy cats that they lifted out of the brook. And so we call them . . .

Pussywillows!

I know a little pussy
Her coat is pearly gray
She lives down in the meadow
Not very far away

She'll always be a pussy
She'll never be a cat
For she's a pussywillow
Now, what do you think of that!

—TRADITIONAL VERSE

Mr. and Mrs. Bird Build a Nest

MEG FISHER

When this story is told as a puppet show, Mr. and Mrs. Bird, made of wool and dangling by looped string from a freshly leafing branch, fly back and forth from their "tree," the puppeteer's lap, to visit their helpful friends. Mrs. Bird is at the tip of the branch so she can get off and sit in the nest later.

SUNG *while birds fly slowly about, to the tune of any standard folk song:*

> *Now at last, winter's past, hear the robin singing!*
> *Now at last, winter's past, spring time bells are ringing!*

SPOKEN:

> *Springtime has come to the valley below.*
> *Gone are the icicles, gone is the snow.*
> *Mr. and Mrs. Bird sit in a tree*
> *Chirp, chirp, chirping merrily.*
> *It's time to build our nest, says she.*
> *Let's go to visit our friend Old Tree.*

SUNG *to the tune of "Good Morning to You":*

> *Good morning, good morning, good morning Old Tree!*

SPOKEN:

> *We're building our nest today.*
> *May we have some of your strong green moss?*
> *Yes, of course you may!*
> *Help yourselves and come back for more!*
> *Thank you, thank you, we are sure!*

SUNG *to your own simple "peck-and-pull" tune:*

With a peck and a pull our beaks are full.
With a peck and a pull our beaks are full.
We're filling our beaks with moss so strong.
We're building and building all day long!

SUNG *(as before):*

Good morning, good morning, good morning, dear Cow!

SPOKEN:

We're building our nest today.
May we have some of your sweet golden hay?
Yes, of course you may!
Help yourselves and come back for more!
Thank you, thank you, we are sure!

SUNG *(as before):*

With a peck and a pull our beaks are full.
With a peck and a pull our beaks are full.
We're filling our beaks with sweet, golden hay.
We're building our nest, our nest today!

Good morning, good morning, good morning, dear Sheep!

SPOKEN:

We're building our nest today.
May we have some of your soft warm wool?
Yes, of course you may!
Help yourselves and come back for more!
Thank you, thank you, we are sure!

SUNG:

With a peck and a pull our beaks are full.
With a peck and a pull our beaks are full.
We're lining our nest with soft, warm wool.
We're building our nest, our nest today!

SPOKEN:

At last the new little nest is done,
Made out of gifts from everyone.
Mrs. Bird sits in the middle of the nest.
Both are tired and need to rest.
Mr. Bird swings on a branch above.
Let's sing a song of thanks, my love!

SUNG:

With a peck and a pull our nest is done.
With a peck and a pull our nest is done.
Thank you, thank you, everyone!
Thank you, thank you, everyone!

∼

OPTIONAL ENDING FOR SECOND WEEK OF PUPPET SHOW

SPOKEN:

A child comes carefully and finds eggs in the tree.

Sing "Spring Secret" or any appropriate springtime song

FINAL VERSE:

The eggs stayed warm and safe and dry
Up in the treetop nest so high.
One day the child heard cheep-cheep-cheep,
So she climbed up to have a peep
And, lo! The baby birds were there
Singing for their supper in the clear spring air!
Papa and Mama fed them all day long
So they would grow up big and strong
And at night they fell asleep to a birdie song.

Hum a closing tune.

RESOURCES

Helen St. John and Daniel Boillat, Mr. and Mrs. Bird and Their Family *(Dornach, Switzerland: Walter Keller Press 1985).*

Mary Thienes Schünemann, "Spring Secret" from Sing a Song of Seasons *(Fairfax, California: Naturally You Can Sing 2005), p. 14.*

The Great Maple

SUSAN SILVERIO

Susan says: "Some kind person offered me this story many years ago for my puppetry at Spindlewood Waldorf Kindergarten on the coast of Maine. It became a favorite! We staged the story at our Seasonal Table, with Maple branches reaching up to receive the sun fairies, and roots extending below the table where the water fairies woke from their sleep and danced up into the trunk. The fairies were simply a small square of silk, tied at the center. With assistance, the children made their own yellow and blue silk fairies and created their own stories with them throughout our long northeastern springtime."

Susan tells this story during maple sap harvesting time, which occurs in late winter in the northeastern United States and Canada. When she brings her class to the trees they've tapped, they share a cup of sap or a taste of syrup. Then they thank the tree with a rhyme, such as "Thank you for this springtime treat. Maple tree, you're lovely sweet."

KING WINTER STILL SITS ON HIS THRONE. The icy winds howl and blow and rattle the branches of the Great Maple tree. It has been a long time since the last leaves fell. When the woodland creatures with full bellies curled up in their caves; when beetles and toads snuggled into the earth; when the root children fell asleep to the gnomes' lullabies . . . it was then that the Great Maple sent its water fairies down into its roots to rest. The gnomes had such a time with those fairies! How they chattered and giggled and wiggled! Often the gnomes had to say, "Shhhh, don't wake the root children. Hush now!"

And so they passed the winter, snug under a blanket of snow.

But up above the earth, the Great Maple stretches into the winter sky. It is cold, quiet, even lonely. In the stillness the maple hears a soft whispering—the faintest, far-off whispering—and listens. It is the moon, telling its long, silvery tales; it is the stars, weaving their secret stories. What marvelous things the tree hears! And though it grows colder and colder, the Great Maple is calm, filled with the joy of these stories. And in the deepest cold of the winter, when the stories are the most wondrous of all, the maple feels a tingling sweetness start in its twigs, then to its branches, and then its trunk, till the Great Maple is filled with sweetness all over. And King Winter on his throne is smiling.

It has been winter for a long time now, and everyone yearns for spring to return. And no one is more excited than the water fairies. Each day they call to the maple tree, "Can we come up now? Are the sun fairies back?" and the Great Maple says, "Not quite yet, but soon I will call you." The poor gnomes! The noisy water fairies have woken some of the root children, who cry out, "May we get up now?" And the gnomes answer, saying, "Hush now; sleep a little longer. You'd get a cold nose if you got up now."

Then one day tired old King Winter falls asleep on his throne. Then how the sun fairies pour out of the heavens—how they rush, warm and bright! The Great Maple holds out its branches to greet them and calls to the water fairies, "The sun fairies are back! Come up!"

Up dance the water fairies, singing a joyful greeting to their beloved sun fairies. The maple tree is so full of happiness that it says to its water fairies, "I have so much sweetness from the winter, won't you each take a bit of it and share it with someone to celebrate the sun fairies' return?" And this they would gladly do, but with whom could they share?

A child comes from her house carrying a bucket, a tap, a cap, and a drill, and stands before the Great Maple. She looks first at the roots, where the snow is beginning to melt, then at the strong trunk. Then she looks at the full, tall crown of the tree and she asks, "May I have some of your sweetness?"

And the tree and all the water fairies say at once, "Oh, yes!"

She carefully drills a hole into the trunk, puts in the tap, and hangs a bucket and cap on it, and out of the trunk drips the sweet sap.

Drip, drip, drip, drip. Wouldn't you like to taste some?

A Flower To Be Found

MARY MANSUR

Mary's love of honeybees, flowers, and children led her to write this story for her kindergarten class. It gave the children a way to help the honeybees!

ONCE UPON A TIME, there was a little girl named Alice who loved flowers. Wherever she went, if there was a flower to be found, she would find it.

One sunny day in early spring, Alice was playing in her yard when she noticed something purple poking its head up through the brown earth. It had been a snowy winter, and even though it was April there were still patches of snow on the ground.

As she got closer, she saw that it was a beautiful purple crocus with a sunny yellow center. "Oh, how beautiful!" thought Alice. "I have to show this to Mother." So Alice picked the crocus and ran with it inside. "Mama," she cried, "This is for you!"

Her mother was at the sink washing the dishes. As she turned around she first noticed Alice's beaming smile, and then she saw the beautiful flower she held in her outstretched hand.

Mother's heart was filled with appreciation for her daughter, for her gift, and for the beautiful flower. "Oh, thank you!" said mother, as she warmly and gently accepted her gift. "It is so beautiful!"

Together, mother and Alice found a vase just the right size, filled it with water, placed the flower in it, and set it on their table.

Alice said, "Oh Mama, the flowers are so beautiful, I'm going to pick them all and give them to you!"

"I'm sure you could," said her mother, "because if there is a flower to be found, you will find it. But did you know that there are hundreds of other little girls in our yard right now who are looking for flowers for their mother?"

Alice ran to the window to look out. She saw her sandbox and the large maple tree. She saw Coal, her grey cat, lounging on the sidewalk soaking up the sun. But she didn't see any people. "Where, Mama? I don't see anyone."

"Let's go take a closer look," said Mother.

So out they went into their yard and Alice led the way to where she had found the flower. There were crocuses and snowdrops and many other flowers just beginning to poke their heads up through the earth.

"Where are the other little girls you were talking about?" asked Alice.

"Hmmmm. . . . Let's stand and watch for a minute and maybe we'll see them," answered Mother.

So Alice and her mother stood enjoying the feel of the warm spring sun on their faces, the gentle spring breeze blowing in their hair, and the sound of the birds singing. It wasn't long before a honeybee lighted on one of the flowers. She took a few steps into the golden center. She moved around and it looked like she was tasting the flower. Sometimes she would take a good long drink. Alice noticed that the honeybee's legs were getting covered with gold.

"This is one of the little girls I was talking about," explained Mother. "She can't bring the whole flower back to her mother, Queen Bee, so she brings the sweetest and tastiest parts. And that flower will have nectar and pollen to share with the bees only as long as it is blooming and growing in the earth."

Just then Alice reached down to pick another flower but stopped when her mother said, "You know Alice, just one single flower is enough to make me happy. But the bees need hundreds and hundreds to make their mother happy. Let's leave the growing flowers for them, and you know what? Whenever you wish to give me a flower, just come get me and share them with me here."

Alice liked that idea and smiled as she watched the honeybee fly up into the air.

"I think we'll be sharing a lot of flowers with these honeybees," she said.

Mama gave Alice a big hug, "I think so, too, because you are very much like them. If there is a flower to be found, you will find it."

Auntie Lila's Garden

ANNIE SOMMERVILLE-HALL

DOWN A LITTLE LANE and past some houses and tall trees there lived a gardener. This old Auntie had been tending her garden for many years, and it had grown. She had fine tall blueberry bushes and fruit trees that were gnarled and squatty, and a large garden full of vegetables, herbs and flowers.

She made sure her plants had rich compost and plenty of water, and that they were planted in just the right places to soak up the sun.

Butterflies and ladybugs loved Auntie Lila's garden. They flew all around adding color and life. They went from plant to plant, flower to flower, and the pollen that went with them helped the flowers and the plants to grow. Bumblebees came to her garden, too. They collected pollen and as they went, their legs became so full of pollen that they almost seemed too heavy to fly.

When Auntie Lila came to check on her blueberries and fruit trees, she could see some fruit starting to grow; small, at first, and then into the summer season, they grew ripe and juicy.

The children who lived nearby loved to visit her. They came with their garden gloves and helped her weed, and dig, and pick the fruit and vegetables.

In the heat of the summer, they came and helped her pick the ripe blueberries. They picked the fruit off the bushes. They brought the blueberries into Auntie Lila's kitchen and helped her make the dough for the pie crust and added the juicy berries. They only made two pies, but OH! they were delicious!

Out in the garden, the butterflies and bumblebees and ladybugs flew from plant to plant. There was a gentle wind and it blew them all into the same area of the garden together.

"How can we help Auntie and her garden?" the butterflies and bumblebees and ladybugs all wondered. "She gives it so much love and attention, but she needs help from the honeybees, too."

They all agreed to spread the word to neighboring gardens and farms and forests that honeybees were welcome and wanted there.

Summer went by and autumn came, with a harvest of a few apples. Winter came and Auntie Lila made sure her plants were bedded down with leaves and mulch.

Spring arrived and new leaves, blossoms, and life came to the garden. One early spring day, Auntie Lila came out to work in her garden and there before her was a swarm of honeybees!

Such a sight! It was a cluster of honeybees looking for a new home. She had a hive! They had arrived! She collected what she needed and came back out to the bees. She laid a sheet carefully out under the swarm. She put an empty hive box right under them. She took a rope and very carefully tied it to the branch where the swarm was clustered all together, buzzing loudly. She took hold of the rope and took a deep breath and then yanked quickly on the rope.

The bees dropped. Some bees went into the box, and some on the sheet, and some on her! She stood very still and watched. There was a small cluster of bees in the box. They were all around the queen bee, taking good care of her. The other bees were marching in a line, one after another, right into the hive box. They looked like a royal parade.

The bees set up house in no time. They had a new home. When all the bees were inside, Auntie put the top on her new hive. Now her garden was so busy! From dawn to dusk the bees went from blossom to blossom, from plant to plant, gathering pollen and nectar and making honey.

The butterflies, bumblebees, and ladybugs were glad for the company. That spring there was more fruit on the trees, more vegetables in the garden, and more blueberries on the bushes than ever before.

In the heat of the summer, the children came to harvest the blueberries and brought their friends. They picked and picked and picked! So many blueberries were brought into the kitchen and so many pies were made, all sweetened with golden honey! OH! They were delicious!

After the children had eaten, they went with Auntie Lila into the garden. They played and sang. The garden hummed and buzzed. The butterflies and ladybugs flew all around. The garden was so much happier with the honeybees and it was especially happy because it was full of children.

Granny Evergreen and Her Gnome Helpers SUSAN STARR

Around 1996, inspired by an AWSNA Conference workshop led by Monique Grund, Susan started making gnome hand puppets. By the end of that year, it was determined that a number of children in her early childhood classroom would go on to first grade, and they needed something fresh and new as they played out their kindergarten days. In three twenty-minute sittings, during outside play time, they sewed on faces and beards, and sewed backs for their hand puppets. Susan let the children name the gnomes according to where the gnomes served in the Plant Kingdom. Then they had short, fun sessions with this story, performing it with their gnomes.

On the last day of kindergarten, with their parents present, the children did this story as a puppet play for their younger classmates. Then off they went to a park for an end-of-year picnic. Parents shared that during those last three weeks their children could not wait to get to school, because "a surprise was coming."

Having these children give a puppet play to their classmates was a culmination: an opportunity for the children going on to first grade to "give back" to the kindergarten, and an opportunity for their powers of imitation to come to fruition.

For this puppet play, Susan also had the children make hammers out of dark blue beeswax for the gnomes, which she put in the freezer to harden before the performance.

SETUP: *The teacher moves a Granny Evergreen puppet. (Susan's Granny Evergreen is a large marionette.) Children with their puppets are behind playstands to the right and left of the teacher—two children per playstand. The playstand shelves should be draped to hide the puppeteers. (Susan used brown fabric to mimic the color of the earth around her classroom.)*

ONCE UPON A TIME, by the edge of the village, there lived an old gardener named Granny Evergreen. Every day Granny Evergreen worked in her garden from dawn to dusk. Summer was coming nigh with many picnics to look forward to, and the great bonfire evening was drawing near.

Granny Evergreen knew her berry pies, fruits, and vegetable were such a delight for all the village families, so she cared for her berries and vegetables especially well. For many winter months, she had made rich compost to feed to her flowers, trees, vegetables, and berry bushes. For some reason there always seemed to be more butterflies in Granny Evergreen's garden than in any of the other village gardens.

Now while Granny Evergreen worked up above, she had many Gnome Helpers who received her rich Mother Earth Compost down below, and they cared for the roots and shoots of her garden. She could not see them, though she longed to—but she knew they were there helping her.

As the teacher calls the names of the various Gnome Hand Puppets, they appear. The names appearing here are only suggestions for the wealth of possible plant names.

Why, there were the Raspberry Patch Gnome, the Strawberry Patch Gnome, and the Blackberry Patch Gnome. And over in the bushes was the Blueberry Bush Gnome.

Granny Evergreen's Pumpkin Patch was just beginning, and there to tend its beginnings was the Pumpkin Patch Gnome.

Granny Evergreen had many fruit trees, and down in the roots were the Plum, Peach and Apricot Gnomes.

The Gnomes hammer on crystals and other interesting rocks..

By the edge of the forest near Granny Evergreen's cottage was a place of wild flowers for the bees. The Forest Gnome kept all in good order there.

Sing to any simple tune:

> *We gnomes, we are digging and delving below*
> *At the roots of berry bushes, flowers and shrubs.*
>
> *We gnomes, we are digging and delving below*
> *With our hammers we knock on the dirt clods and stones.*

One evening as the sun was setting, Granny Evergreen was having a cup of tea and looking out over her beautiful garden after a day's work. She had forgotten her shawl, when suddenly a cool breeze came into the garden and gave Granny Evergreen a cold chill.

That night, as Granny Evergreen sat on her bed, she felt her cheeks warm and said, "Oh my, I feel a fever coming on." She lay down, and all night long, she baked a good fever.

Early the next morning, when the gnomes did not hear the familiar pitter-patter of Granny Evergreen's feet up above, it was decided that two gnomes should go up above to investigate.

Two Gnomes, one from each side of the teacher, approach Granny Evergreen.

Carefully, Strawberry and Apricot Gnome tiptoed into Granny Evergreen's house, and when they saw her fast asleep, and her cheeks as red as strawberries, they said, "We must help Granny Evergreen."

Strawberry Gnome said, "I will ask my friends to go and get some chamomile from the meadow fairies."

Apricot Gnome said, "I will ask my friends to visit the Queen of the Bees and ask for some of her honey."

So they each took a basket and bucket and set out.

The children pass a bucket along the front of one playstand to Apricot Gnome. All repeat, "Pass the bucket . . ."

It was announced to all the gnomes that Granny Evergreen was not well and needed chamomile and honey.

When the bucket got to Blueberry Patch Gnome, he went into the woods and visited the wild bee hive there, and asked, "Queen of the Bees, Queen of the Bees, Granny Evergreen has a fever and can we have some of your honey to take to her?"

The Queen of the Bees came out of her hive and replied, "I know Granny Evergreen's garden very well. My bees delight in her fruit and vegetable blossoms. Here, take as much as you need."

The teacher has a strip of golden silk prepared for the Queen of Bees to "pour" into a bucket. (Susan uses a small basket shaped like a beehive to "pour from.")

"Thank you," said the Blueberry Gnome.

The children pass the bucket back along the front of the first playstand to Strawberry Gnome, repeating, "Pass the honey bucket . . ."

"Pass the basket," said Apricot Gnome.

Along the other playstand, the children pass a basket to Apricot Gnome, repeating, "Pass the basket . . ." The teacher speaks the name of the last Gnome, who will take the basket to meet Lady Chamomile.

The last Gnome walked into the meadow saying, "Lady Chamomile, Lady Chamomile, Granny Evergreen is not well and needs some fresh chamomile flowers."

Lady Chamomile replied, "I know Granny Evergreen's garden very well. We fairies delight in all her flowers. Here are many chamomile flowers, freshly picked this morning."

The last Gnome thanked her and returned to the garden.

Children pass the last Gnome's basket along the playstand back to Apricot Gnome, repeating "Pass the chamomile basket . . ."

Carefully, the two gnomes put all their gifts by the back porch and returned down below, where all the gnomes patiently waited.

Granny Evergreen sat up from her bed, and said to herself, "I will need a good cup of tea after such a night."

When she looked out on her porch, there to her surprise was just what she needed.

"I wonder where these helpful gifts came from?" she said.

She made herself a nice cup of tea with honey, and with her shawl on, she sat outside. "I will not be able to work in my garden today, but I will delight in its beauty," she said.

And then something happened.

With her fever, Granny Evergreen's eyes were opened a little more than usual, and now she could see all the gnomes and fairies waving at her and working well.

She knew then where the gifts had come from.

And she knew that her helpers would care for her garden that day, while she watched and rested.

We gnomes, we are digging and delving below
At the roots of berry bushes, flowers and shrubs.

We gnomes, we are digging and delving below
With our hammers we knock on the dirt clods and stones.

Stories for Autumn Time

Seed Babies

JOANNE DENNEE, ADAPTED FROM A STORY BY MARY LOOMIS GAYLORD

An early- to mid-fall story for lap puppetry. This makes a good protection story, using silks and gauzes for the different elements. It can even be done in the round, on children's laps, having pairs of older children moving the elements or passing them one to another.

A H, ME," SAID MOTHER AUTUMN, as she cradled her seed babies in her lap, embracing them with a layer of leaves. "So many flowers are turning into seeds. The seed babies will need a cozy blanket for the earth cradle to warm them until spring is here again. Father Sun's spark is resting deep inside each seed baby. The Good Gnomes and I shall protect them. I wonder, what kind of blanket shall it be? I must find something. Let me see. Hmmmm...it should be something soft and light. And for babies, of course."

So she called to Brother Wind and said:

> *"Oh, Brother Wind, please bring to me*
> *A blanket that's just right.*
> *Soft as down and sparkling bright,*
> *To wrap my little seed babies,*
> *That they do not shiver and freeze."*

But Brother Wind said, "I cannot unless Jack Frost will give me some of his silvery powder."

So Mother Autumn called to Jack Frost: "Oh, Jack Frost, please give Brother Wind some of your silvery powder."

> *"Oh, Frost, and Wind, please bring to me*
> *A blanket silvery powder light,*
> *Soft as down and sparkling bright,*
> *To wrap my little seed babies,*
> *That they do not shiver and freeze."*

But Jack Frost said: "You must ask the Cloud Sisters to give me some vapor, then."

So Mother Autumn called to the clouds and said: "Cloud Sisters, please give to Jack Frost some of your vapor, that he may change it into silvery powder and give it to Brother Wind.

> *"Oh, Clouds and Frost, please bring to me*
> *A blanket fluffy and white,*
> *Soft as down and sparkling bright,*
> *To wrap my little seed babies,*
> *That they do not shiver and freeze."*

But the Cloud Sisters said: "We must wait until Grandmother Ocean sends us even more vapor."

So Mother Autumn said to Grandmother Ocean: "Please, Grandmother Ocean, send more vapor to the Cloud Sisters, that they may give some to Jack Frost, that he may change it into silvery powder and give it to Brother Wind."

> *"Oh, Grandmother Ocean and Clouds, please bring to me*
> *A blanket blue and light,*
> *Soft as down and sparkling bright,*
> *To wrap my little seed babies,*
> *That they do not shiver and freeze."*

But Grandmother Ocean said: "Father Sun must send me some sunbeams first."

So Mother Autumn said to Father Sun: "Dear Father Sun, please send some of your sunbeams to Grandmother Ocean, that she may send some vapor to the Clouds, that they may give some to Jack Frost, that he may change it into silvery powder and give it to Brother Wind."

"Oh, Father Sun and Grandmother Ocean, please bring to me
A blanket gold with light,
Soft as down and sparkling bright,
To wrap my little seed babies,
That they do not shiver and freeze."

And so they all did.

Mother Autumn was so pleased to receive such help from Father Sun, Grandmother Ocean, the Cloud Sisters, Jack Frost and Brother Wind.

"Now the seed babies can rest warm in my lap," she said, "beneath these blankets pure and bright. Ah! I see Old Man Winter is here to play and has brought a quilt of snow to lay."

"Oh, seed babies now rest close to me
Beneath these blankets pure and bright,
Soft as down and sparkling bright,
Winter's snow quilt is certain to please,
And protect you...you will not shiver and freeze."

Sing "Sleep, Baby, Sleep" or other appropriate lullaby. The storyteller can alter the lyrics to mention seeds instead of human babies, such as "Sleep, little seeds, sleep . . ."

RESOURCES

"Sleep, Baby, Sleep," German traditional. See the Metropolitan Museum of Art, Lullabies: An Illustrated Songbook *(New York: Gulliver Books 1997), p. 18.*

Grampsy's Apple Walk

ANDREE WARD

Andree gratefully attributed to Suzanne Down the idea of having a local forest dweller (Grampsy Tomten) appear in lots of stories involving our local flora and fauna. This was her first such story, introducing Grampsy and some of his friends, who would appear in later stories and who actually lived in her classroom, in the form of knitted animals.

On days that Andree tells this story, the children begin the morning polishing apples. After the performance, each child can take an apple home, perhaps wrapped in a red napkin.

GRAMPSY TOMTEN LIVES IN A COZY HOME under the oldest oak tree in the forest on Banjo Mountain. He likes to take a long walk every morning to see what he can see and to visit with his many friends. He usually returns home with an interesting story to tell. But first we will have to wake him up.

Sing to any simple mood-of-the-fifth tune:

> *Good morning, Grampsy Tomten*
> *Will you come out, please?*
> *Come tell us a story,*
> *Tell us, won't you please?*
> *(Repeat)*

When Grampsy woke up this morning, he looked out his window and saw that Jack Frost had come to the forest. He thought to himself, "What a beautiful autumn day! The sun is shining bright. And Mother Apple Tree always sweetens her apples after Jack Frost visits. Maybe she has let some of them drop to the ground. I'll just take my basket and go for a walk."

And because he was so happy, he sang his walking song.

Sing to any simple tune:

> *Hey Ho, Hey Ho!*
> *And always I go*
> *A-walking along*
> *And singing my song.*
> *Hey Ho, Hey Ho!*

When Grampsy got to Mother Apple Tree, sure enough, there were many apples on the ground—and many more ripening up in her branches. "Oh, good," said Grampsy, "I'll just pick up a few and see if any of my friends would like one." So Grampsy filled his basket and started walking back home.

Now here came one of Grampsy's friends, Grumbly Bear. Grumble, grumble, bumble, bumble, Bear came down the path.

"Good morning, Grumbly Bear. Would you like to eat a ripe, red, juicy apple, the first of the season?"

"Good morning, Grampsy. Why, yes, I would love a nice ripe apple. You are very kind to share your apples with me. Thank you."

"Oh, Bear, Mother Apple Tree has many more for us," said Grampsy. And Grumbly Bear walked off with his apple, humming a grumbly, bumbly song.

The next friend to come along was Frisky Fox. "Good morning, Frisky Fox. How would you like a sweet apple, freshly picked?"

"Well, I would love to eat a sweet apple. That's very kind of you, Grampsy. Thank you." And Frisky Fox went scampering off to his den with his lovely ripe apple.

The next friend to come along was Hop-Along Bunny. "Good morning, Hop-Along. How would you like a sweet apple for your mid-morning snack?"

"Well, thank you very much, Grampsy. A sweet apple would be very tasty right now." And Hop-Along Bunny went hopping along home with his shiny red apple.

By now, Grampsy was very near his cozy home down under the roots of the oldest oak tree. Sitting high up in the tree was Grampsy's friend, the wise old owl. "Good morning, Owl. What are you doing way up there?"

"Well, Grampsy, I've been taking a lovely nap on this fine autumn day."

"Would you like a sweet apple? I have one left."

"Oh, no, Grampsy, I have been eating Mother Apple Tree's sweet apples all morning. That's why I needed a nap! I think that last apple is for you!"

"Hm-m-m," said Grampsy, "I think you are right." And Grampsy popped that sweet apple into his pocket.

Now Owl asked, "Grampsy, have you told the children about the secret that Mother Apple Tree has hidden inside each of her apples?"

"Well, no, I haven't told them yet," said Grampsy.

"Then I think it's time to tell them."

Grampsy now addresses his audience.

"Well, children, here is a wonderful secret. Down deep inside each apple, Mother Apple Tree has hidden a lovely surprise. It is a secret star to remind you of your own star up in Heaven, the star you just came from. So when you cut open an apple, you will see a star inside, with many baby apple seeds sleeping in their star cradles. When you see them, remember the secret of the apple star and the twinkling stars up in Heaven."

While the storyteller cuts open an apple, all can sing "Twinkle, Twinkle, Little Star" or another appropriate, familiar song.

Mrs. Mouse and the Maple Leaf

KELLY MARIE BARHAM

ONE GOLDEN AUTUMN MORNING, a little child went for a walk in the forest. Dry leaves crackled under his feet, and the sky was blue above him.

He stopped to pick up little stones and acorns and put them into fairy moss gardens.

He saw a stick that he liked, and decided to go fishing. Then he raked leaves for a while. And then—he whacked his stick on the trunk of a tall maple tree. He liked the way it sounded, BUT. . . .

Mrs. Mouse, who lived between the roots of the tree, was frightened. She didn't like the noise, and she didn't know what was making her little house shake, so she ran out her door and straight up to the top of the tree.

She was so happy when she looked down and saw that it was just a little child playing.

And she was also happy when he put the stick down and went skipping off. He didn't even know that he had frightened Mrs. Mouse right out of her house.

Mrs. Mouse looked around and saw that she was up higher than she had ever been before! She could see mountains far, far away. She could see the golden grain growing in Farmer Brown's field.

"What a beautiful sight!" she said to herself. "But now I must get back to my cozy home between the roots."

Then, Mrs. Mouse looked down—and saw how far she had to go. And her little pink paws trembled.

"How will I get down?" she asked herself. "It's much too far to jump. Is there no one who can help me?"

Nearby, a friendly maple leaf heard her and waved. "Mrs. Mouse, I am on my way down. Would like to ride on my back?" asked Maple Leaf.

"Oh yes! What a kind friend you are, dear Maple Leaf."

Mrs. Mouse climbed carefully onto the leaf, and together they floated down to Mother Earth.

Maple Leaf was so happy to be with its brothers and sisters. And Mrs. Mouse scampered off to her cozy home between the roots.

The Hungry Dragon

LISA STOESSEL

A Michaelmas story for the nursery.

ONCE UPON A TIME there was a little girl who lived with her mother close by an apple orchard. She loved to play among the apple trees all year long. In the spring, she would pick the daffodils that grew among the roots of the apple trees, and she would watch the caterpillars wind their cocoons. In the summer she would climb into the trees and hide among the leaves. There was a special tree that had a big curving branch that made the most wonderful nook for her to nestle in. There she would watch the clouds float by in the soft blue sky. In the autumn she would pick the apples, bushels full of apples, and take them home to her mother. They would make applesauce, apple pies, baked apples and even dried apples that would hang from the rafters. In the winter, when the trees were bare, she would pretend they were so many children holding their arms up to the sky, waiting for the snow to fall. And when it did, she would make a snowman just beside her favorite tree, to keep it company.

One day in the early autumn, the little girl went with her mother to pick apples in the orchard. It was a clear and breezy day, and her mother let her bring a beautiful shiny kite to fly in the clearing. When the little girl grew tired of picking apples, she asked her mother if she could fly her kite. Her mother said, "Yes, but hold on tight; there's quite a breeze coming along." So the little girl stood back some distance from the trees and lifted her kite into the wind. It didn't take long before the playful wind took it up and the kite sailed off above the treetops.

It was a lovely day, and the little girl had so much fun watching her kite dance in the sky, to and fro. After some time, a few clouds began to roll in and the little girl and her mother heard some rumbling off in the distance. They wondered whether there might be some rain coming along.

Well, the wind changed, and all of a sudden the kite went sailing out of her hand and off into the sky! The little girl watched in dismay as her kite went higher and higher up into the clouds. Her mother said, "Sometimes kites seem to have a mind of their own, and they decide to go for an adventure. We'll make another one when we get home." The little girl munched on an apple as she thought about her kite having a grand adventure up in the wild blue yonder.

Then something very surprising happened! All of the sudden the sky grew dark, the wind became wild, and that rumbling noise got louder and closer! As the little girl and her mother looked up, they saw a dragon circling in the sky above them! And what was even more amazing was that he was holding the little girl's kite in his talons! Slowly, slowly he came down through the trees and landed right there in the apple orchard.

The little girl was quite frightened, but the dragon spoke, saying, "Hello there! I had gone up for a little flight around the mountains and I spotted this beautiful kite, which was having quite an adventure. I thought someone might be missing it. Is it yours?"

The little girl replied that it was indeed and she thanked him as he gave it back to her. The little girl's mother asked how they might repay his kindness, and he replied that all that flying had given him quite an appetite. The little girl said, "You can have some of our delicious apples!" That pleased the dragon, and he had a delightful snack of apples.

All of a sudden that rumbling noise stopped, for all that noise had come from the dragon's empty stomach. Now it was full, so he was happy. And the little girl got her beautiful kite back, so she was happy. And the dragon took up the big basket of apples for the mother and flew it back to the house, so the mother was happy. And so, of course, they all lived happily ever after.

The Golden Cape of Courage

CANDICE ACHENBACH

Another Michaelmas story to share with young children.

ONCE THERE WAS A LITTLE BOY who lived with his mother and father on a small farm at the edge of town. One evening, his father stayed late working in his shop in the middle of town, and his mother bid him take some supper to his father.

Now, the boy had gone alone to town to visit his father's shop many times before, and in fact, he passed by the shop on his way to and from school each day. But all these times the sun was shining, and he could easily see what was around him. Now, all around was dark, for the sun had gone to bed long ago. The boy was worried about what might be hiding in the darkness and whether or not he would be able to find his way on the dark path. His mother assured him that his lantern would shine light on the path, so he could find his way, and that everything along the path would be the same as it had been that afternoon.

Before the boy set off, his mother fastened his golden cape around his shoulders. He remembered how his grandmother had made it for him last fall, just after the King's Knights had ridden through town in a grand parade, wearing their sparkling golden armor. He thought to himself that if the Knights' golden armor could keep them safe in battle, then surely his golden cape would keep him safe on his walk to town. As the boy set out on his journey into town, his cape kept him warm, and his lantern shone brightly on the path.

After he had traveled along a bit, he was startled by a noise, so much so that he almost dropped the basket with his father's supper. As he stood frozen, listening to the sound, he soon realized that it was Chloe and Clyde Cricket, who sang outside his bedroom window each night. He felt a little sleepy listening to their song, but quickly remembered his task and continued on his way.

When he was almost to the middle of town, he was again startled by a noise, so much so that he almost dropped his lantern. He stood frozen for a moment, until he realized that the sound was a voice he knew. It was Old Rufus the dog, who belonged to Mistress Fisher down the lane. He called out, "Good Evening, Old Rufus!"

He soon found the way to his father's shop. Again he stopped for a moment, startled by how dark the shop window was, and he wondered if perhaps his father was not inside. But as he peered in, he saw a small candle flickering in the back of the shop. His father was so glad to see him, and very thankful for the supper in his basket.

Father was just finishing up his work for the night. The boy sat with him while he ate. And then the two together returned home. The lantern lit their way home, past Old Rufus, past the crickets, and right into their little farmhouse, where Mother had warm beds waiting for both of them.

The Princess and the Dragon

SHARIFA OPPENHEIMER

For this Michaelmas story in verse, Sharifa offers song suggestions to be interspersed with the spoken text, but storytellers are encouraged to find or create their own.

Once upon a time in a far-away land
There lived a king in a castle grand.
The king was kind and wise and good,
He cared for his people as a good king should.

The good king's land spread far and wide,
His daughter, the princess, was by his side.
Of all of that which gave him pleasure,
His daughter, the princess, was his greatest treasure.

Each year at harvest time, in the fall,
The farmers came to the castle tall,
Bringing apples, carrots and grain,
Grown with the help of sun and rain.

Then the people would celebrate
The gifts of the harvest, small and great!
So the people prospered, year after year,
Living in joy, with nothing to fear.

Sing "Harvest Crown" or any harvest song:

> Harvest crown we are weaving,
> We weave the harvest crown.
> Now our [child's name] shall be the weaver,
> And our [child's name] too.

Continue with spoken verse:

> Alas, great sorrow fell on the land.
> One year the farmers came with empty hands.
> "A fiery dragon has burned our crops,
> He burns our huts; at nothing he stops."

> Said the king, "I will vanquish him with my might.
> I will send my sturdy knight,
> With sword of iron in his hand
> To sweep this terror from our land."

> The knight donned armor, sword and mail.
> At his task he would not fail.
> Away from the castle he bravely rode;
> He would not stop till the dragon's abode.

Sing "I Am Riding," or any Michaelmas riding song. Continue with verse:

> But at the dragon's fiery blast
> His sword was melted down to the last.
> The knight returned, his spirits lagging.
> The king said, "I will speak to the dragon."

Sing a Michaelmas riding song. Continue with verse:

> Said the king: "I have known many a dragon of old.
> You steal jewels, treasures and gold.
> I will give you all our treasure,
> If you will leave us to our pleasure."

> Said the dragon: "For treasures and gold I do not care;
> All I want is the princess fair."

"Never, indeed!" sang the king's refrain.
Hissed the dragon, "Then I'll burn up all your grain!"

The king returned, his heart was broken.
Quickly, though, the princess had spoken;
"Of heaven's help I can be sure.
Heaven helps those whose hearts are pure."

The people did weep, the king did moan,
The princess would face the dragon alone!
Alone and fair, dressed in white,
The princess would face the dragon's might.

Sing "We Walk Toward You," or any Michaelmas rejoicing song. Continue with verse:

Closer and closer came the dragon's fire;
The princess looked toward heaven higher,
When out from the clouds with lightning speed
Rushed an angel on a wind-bred steed,

Brandishing a glittering sword.
In mortal fear the dragon roared.
No sword of earthly iron held he,
But heavenly iron the princess could see.

One touch of Michael's sword aflame,
And the dragon's beastly heart was tame!
Said the dragon, "Now no more will my terror spread,
I'll fire your ovens to make your bread!"

The people rejoiced, and they did sing.
And Michael's voice did ring:
"Of Heaven's help we can be sure;
Heaven helps those whose hearts are pure."

And so they lived happily ever after.

Sing a Michaelmas rejoicing song.

RESOURCES

"Harvest Crown," Traditional. See, e.g., Nancy Foster, editor, Dancing as We Sing *(Silver Spring, Maryland: Acorn Hill Nursery 1999) p. 14, sung to end a Harvest Circle.*

Traditional, largely unpublished material for Michaelmas circle play in the Waldorf early childhood classroom is passed from teacher to teacher. Useful resources are nevertheless available in print and online. See, e.g., Nancy Foster, editor, The Seasonal Festivals in Early Childhood *(Chestnut Ridge, New York: Waldorf Early Childhood Association of North America 2010) p. 31; Betty Jones,* A Child's Seasonal Treasury *(Chestnut Ridge, New York: Waldorf Early Childhood Association of North America 2018) p. 33; and the "Michaelmas" album at Cincinatti Waldorf Songbook, cincinnatiwaldorfsongbook.bandcamp.com/album/ michaelmas.*

Dragon Tears

MARY CARIDI-GORGA

ONCE UPON A TIME in a kingdom far away, there lived a dragon. She was rather pretty with scales of green and yellow that shone bright and pleasant. She lived in a cave by the water, and although she wasn't particularly friendly with the people of the village, neither was she unfriendly.

She was also rather lazy, sleeping away most of the morning like a big cat. Around lunch time, she would finally awaken, yawning and stretching. Before long she'd launch herself into the air, flying off to hunt for food in the wilderness. After she had eaten and felt a little more energetic, she would fly above the kingdom, beating her great wings and racing against the wind.

On nice days, the dragon would make a pass over the village rather close to the ground, for she loved to see the people point up at her, and hear them admiring her beauty. Sometimes she would even do a flip in the air, and the people would exclaim and clap. The scales that covered her back and wings were a deep emerald green, while the golden ones on her chest and tummy shone so brightly in the sun that they were dazzling. She was quite an impressive sight to behold, and she was very proud of her good looks.

She began to grow reckless, however, and when she hunted for food, she would sometimes accidentally trample on people's farms. When this happened, she didn't bother to stop and make things right. She just went on her way. Upset with her for her carelessness, the people stopped cheering when they saw her flying.

When the people no longer cheered, the dragon was confused and annoyed. You see, she was actually kind of shy. She didn't really know how to be with people, if you can believe it. So, after a short time, she grew cross and became more reckless and just a little bit mean, sometimes trampling fields on purpose, just to show people that she didn't care what they thought. The more reckless she became, the more people grew afraid of her, so they began to turn away when they saw her, and shake their heads.

The dragon told herself that she didn't care. She stayed in her cave longer and longer, and came out to hunt later and later in the day. One day, the dragon didn't wake up until nearly dinner time. She stretched and emerged from her dark cave and flew off to the wilderness to hunt. But on her way back to the village, she noticed something very unusual happening in the sky. You see, the dragon hadn't ever been awake late enough to see a sunset before. She had never seen the way the sun paints the sky and clouds with such amazing colors. Gold, deep orange, and bright crimson shone all along the western sky. Instead of rejoicing in the beauty she saw, the dragon was filled with jealousy.

She wanted to be the prettiest thing in the skies! She was worried that nobody would even notice her flying in the sky when the sunset was so beautiful. And the colors kept changing and grew more beautiful as she watched.

The dragon started to roar angrily as she flew, demanding that the sun stop it right now! But the sun just continued to shine and be beautiful. What else could it be?

Now the dragon was livid with anger. She didn't care that it was her own fault that she had made herself unpopular. She didn't care about doing the right thing. She was so angry that all she saw was red, and for the first time she began to bellow ugly smoke and flames from her mouth. She was so surprised that she almost fell from the skies! The flames burnt her face, and the noxious smoke was terrible to breathe. But it did feel good to roar so loudly, so she did it again, and flapped her wings furiously and flew higher than she'd ever been.

The sun continued to paint the sky, however, and the colors spread, and spanned the whole rim of the sky, so that even the clouds in the eastern sky were turning pink and lavender. Well, the dragon became even more angry and upset. Now her yelling turned into screaming, with red flickering flames which whipped all around her body, scorching her scales until they were charred and dark. The more she screamed and bellowed out fire and insults, the uglier she became, and of course the uglier she became, the angrier she felt.

Down below, the people gathered together, frightened by what they saw. There were many brave people among them, but they did not know how they were going to protect themselves if the dragon came swooping down upon them. There was one little girl, however, who remembered that if you needed help, you should ask for it. So she sang a small song of courage, and cried out for help.

Up in the heavens lived the Archangel Michael. He heard the dragon's screams and the little girl's song of courage. Although he lived so far away, he wanted to help the people in some way. So, he sent down his shooting stars of iron bright . . .

SONG:

The dragon was flying so high, so high,
Jealous of the sun in the sky.
The sun was setting orange and red.
The dragon cried, "Look at me instead!"

The sunset was such a lovely sight
With gold and bronze and crimson bright.
The dragon roared, "I'll fight, I'll fight!
I don't care if it's wrong or right!"

"Oh Michael, we call to you,
We know your heart is brave and true!"
And Michael, so filled with light
Sent shooting stars of iron bright.

The sun just shone with majesty.
The dragon had to turn and flee.
The shooting stars of iron bright
Pursued the dragon through the night.

Like swords the stars of iron were,
Driving the dragon down to the earth.
Oh Michael and Shooting Stars
Bring us courage from afar.

Michael's shooting stars drove the dragon down closer and closer to the earth, and the stardust fell upon her and clogged up her nose and eyes and made it hard for her to see. She was still very angry, but there was nothing more she could do. The shooting stars drove her down from the sky, and at last she was forced back to her cave. She crawled inside in the darkness, laid down and curled up. All at once, she began to cry big dragon tears.

Now as you may know, dragon's tears are very rare and carry magic in them. But these dragon tears were even more special, for they were mixed with the magic of Michael's shooting stars. As she cried, her tears streamed down over her soot-stained wings and body, and began to wash away the smoke and grime that had covered her when she was screaming and shooting out flames. She cried for a very long time, for underneath all her anger she was actually very sad. When at last she stopped crying, and had only a few little hiccups left, she quietly wiped her snout and her eyes with her paws, put her head down, and fell asleep.

The townspeople had watched the shooting stars falling from the sky and had seen the dragon return to her cave. They sent up a song of thanks to Michael and went to sleep hopeful that tomorrow would be a better day.

The little girl who had called out for Michael's help got up early the next morning. She loved to watch the sky go from black to a deep magical blue and hear the birds singing in longing for the sun to rise. As she made her way through the village, she saw the sun painting the sky again with beautiful pinks, purples, and pale yellows. Then she noticed something strange. There were bright flashes of gold and green on the hillside near the dragon's cave! She carefully crept closer to the cave and saw that the beautiful green and golden light was coming from inside the cave.

Curious, she crawled to the very edge of the entrance and peeked inside. There, she saw that the brilliant lights she had seen flashing on the hillside belonged to the dragon, whose scales of green and yellow shone and danced like sparkling ripples in a stream on a sunny day. The girl cried out in wonder, and was drawn closer to the dragon and her brilliant colors. So taken was she by the beautiful lights that she followed them right into the dragon's cave. Then she stretched out her hand to touch the scales, and laughed in delight.

The dragon, though she was lying very still, had awoken when the girl entered the cave, and was watching her from underneath her eyelids. When the little girl softly touched her, the dragon felt confused, scared, warm, and hopeful all at the same time. "Why is she here?" wondered the dragon, who did not know that all her ugliness had washed away in her tears. And when the girl began to laugh so sweetly and started petting the dragon and cooing to her, the dragon could stand it no longer, and opened her eyes to see what was going on.

She blinked her eyes three times in surprise when she saw that her ruined paws and wings and belly were now gleaming and brilliant. The little girl watched the dragon's face light up with delight, so that when at last the dragon looked at her again, they were both smiling great big smiles.

The dragon and the girl became good friends. Now they both woke early in the morning to see the sun rise and listen to the birds sing. The girl brought the dragon to the fields where the dragon worked hard with her strong claws and spiky tail to repair and re-plow the fields that she had trampled in her carelessness, so that now the fields could be re-planted with the help of the villagers. As for the little girl, she often went riding on the dragon's back. She helped the dragon become friendly with the other children in the village and give them rides so that the sky was filled with singing and laughter.

But the favorite thing that the dragon and the girl did together was to launch into the air when the sun was setting and fly up among the clouds as the sun painted colors across the sky.

And if things have not changed, then they are still the same today.

The Pumpkin House

KATHY FRASER

The inspiration for this verse came from a story that Cynthia Lambert and Karen Viani used in leading "Fundamentals of the Waldorf Kindergarten," a workshop at Rudolf Steiner College in 2009.

In the autumn garden grew a pumpkin, round and gold;
Along came a mousie, shivering in the cold.
"Little mouse, where's your house? Winter's coming soon.
Little mouse, find a house—be snug by Harvest Moon!"

Nibble, nibble went the mouse, until the pumpkin was a house,
With two high windows and a big wide door,
And softest feathers on the floor.
There she stayed, snug and warm, safe through every winter storm.

Through the field on jumping feet, came a cricket, looking for a house so neat.
Across the way, he sees a glow: it's Mousie's house! "Hello! Hello!"
Just then the North Wind blew, and chilled that cricket through and through.
He said, "May I move in with you?"

Mousie peeped out, and said "Yes, you may,
and through the coming winter stay."
And so they lived snug and warm,
safe through every winter storm.

Through the field on long, thin feet, came a spider, looking for a house so neat.
Across the way, he sees a glow: it's Mousie's house! "Hello! Hello!"
Just then the North Wind blew, and chilled that spider through and through.
He said, "May I move in with you?"

Mousie peeped out, and said "Yes, you may,
and through the coming winter stay."
And so they lived snug and warm,
safe through every winter storm.

Through the field on big, soft feet, came a bear, looking for a house so neat.
Across the way, he sees a glow: it's Mousie's house! "Hello! Hello!"
Just then the North Wind blew, and chilled that bear through and through.
He said, "May I move in with you?"

Mousie, cricket, and spider too, said,
"Oh dear! What shall we do?
Our house is much too small for you!"

Bear thought: "Hmmmmmmmmmmm.
Then under these leaves I'll make my bed
and I'll stay here beside you instead."

And so they lived snug and warm, safe through every winter storm.

Now the pumpkin is a house,
lived in by spider, cricket, and mouse.
Like bear, beside them we may stay,
until we make our homeward way.

A Halloween Pumpkin Story

NANCY FORER

THERE ONCE WAS a mother, a father, a brother, and a sister. They loved to tend their garden.

Each Spring they prepared the soil.
They raked it clean and fine.
They planted seeds
and watered them well.
They pulled out all the weeds.
Each day they watched for what would grow.

The summer sun warmed the skies and soil, and ever so slowly the garden began to sprout . . .

a little leaf here . . .

and another one there,

until a strong green vine spread itself out, ever so fine.

The children watered that vine and watched it grow.

By and by a beautiful golden blossom unfolded.
Oh how the children loved it so!

Mother and father told them,
"We must not pick this blossom, but let it flower and grow.
Many days and lots of nights will come and will go.
When at last Father Sun makes short our days
and Autumn winds begin to blow
Our garden's blossom will have something new to show."

The children continued to tend the garden well each day.
They pulled out the weeds,
watered it ever so carefully,
and then went about their play,
leaving the blossom to grow quietly in its own way.

Many days and lots of nights passed
and cool Autumn winds began to blow.
Mother, father, brother and sister went walking in the garden . . .

and *Oh!*

There on the vine, where the blossom had grown, sat an orange pumpkin,
with the brightest glow.

"Dear children," said Papa, "Your work is well done.
You've waited long and patiently.
This pumpkin's the one!
It's grown so big and round and fine.
It's time to take it from its vine."

They carried that pumpkin home . . . carefully.
The children were so happy, they danced with glee!

Mama said, "With this big pumpkin, there's much we can do.
We'll make pie, roast the seeds, and carve a jack-o-lantern, too!"

Then she said, "Cut into the pumpkin!"

Say the poem "Cut into the Pumpkin":

> *Scoop it with a spoon*
> *Carve a little mouth*
> *The shape of a moon.*
> *Make two eyes to twinkle*
> *And a big, three-cornered nose.*
> *And for teeth, some shiny seeds*
> *Placed all in a row.*

When all was ready, a little candle was lit
and carefully placed inside the pumpkin.
Now it became a jack-o-lantern!

Sing "Jack-o-Lantern" song:

> *Jack-o-lantern, Jack-o-lantern*
> *How your light it does shine*
> *Sitting up upon the window*
> *and your light it does shine.*
>
> *You were once an orange pumpkin*
> *Sitting on a pumpkin vine*
> *Now you are my Jack-o-lantern*
> *and your little light is mine.*

RESOURCES

"Cut into a Pumpkin" from Jennifer Aulie and Margret Meyerkort, Autumn *(Stourbridge, England: Wynstones Press 1999).*

"Jack-o-Lantern" from Mary Thienes Schünemann, Sing a Song of Seasons *(Fairfax, California: Naturally You Can Sing 2005).*

Old Grandmother Pumpkin

JOANNE DENNEE

This makes for a lovely outdoor Halloween vignette. Joanne's class always experienced this as a play in the forest when the children went for a Halloween walk—only to discover Old Grandmother Pumpkin sweeping. Miniature Jack-Be-Little Pumpkins were scattered about the leaf litter. The year that Old Grandmother Pumpkin could not make it for the performance, the class still stumbled upon her broom and rocking chair, and a little cup of warm tea set upon a tree stump. Told that Old Grandmother must be further off in the forest, "searching for the spark in the seeds," the class knew just what to do to help—they left behind little gnome houses so she would know they'd been there. They left with their pumpkins carefully cradled in their arms. In the days that followed, the class returned and each placed a pumpkin seed in a gnome house for the busy gnomes to guard. When they returned yet again, Old Grandmother Pumpkin and the Good Gnomes had gathered the seeds one and all.

THERE SHE WAS, the Old Pumpkin Grandmother, busy working in the forest, sweeping with her broom, sweeping away the leaves in search of something. Along came some children to gather up acorns and rainbow leaves.

As the children came closer they heard her say, "Oh dear, I know those pumpkin seeds must be here somewhere. But I can't remember where I left them."

Sweep, sweep, sweep. She was so busy with that broom of hers!

"They are not inside my seed pouch," she sighed. She gazed down into the darkest corners of her pouch and then, fretting, she shook it upside down, hoping those little seeds would fall out into her hands. But nothing seemed to be clinging inside. "Well, I'd better look over there."

Sweep, sweep, sweep. Soon she had made a giant pile of leaves—so high it was!

"This is getting very tiring and very worrisome," she said. "I must start gathering the pumpkin seeds for next year's pumpkin babies, or Jackie Frost will nip them with his icy fingers. The gnomes are waiting to help me too, but I just can't seem to find a single seed. At night the seeds sparkle, with the last light from Father Sun hidden inside them. But during the day they are so hard to find."

Sweep, sweep, sweep. "Oh dear, if I just had some help."

"Oh," said the children, who had been watching so quietly. "We are very good helpers. Can we help you?" All the children started sweeping their hands through the fallen leaves. There were leaves of every color—red, orange, yellow, gold, brown. Yet not one child could find a pumpkin seed anywhere!

Then one child asked to look in Old Grandmother's seed pouch. Old Grandmother Pumpkin said, "Certainly, just be sure to check the darkest corners. Seeds love the darkness of Mother Earth."

The child was so eager to help Grandmother Pumpkin. She stretched the seed pouch open wide, then peered inside. Alas, no seeds there!

Another helpful child picked up an old wrinkled pumpkin gourd that was sitting close by. She rattled it. Then she rattled it again. Looking surprised she asked, "What can that sound be? I wonder!"

Old Grandmother Pumpkin came closer to listen. She put her ear to the sound. Then she let out a funny little laugh.

"Oh, how silly of me! Look around. There are pumpkin seeds everywhere. I did put them in a special place. Now I remember, I planted them in Mother Earth and now they are all hiding inside the little pumpkins. But, oh, what will I do? I do not have enough time to carve all these in time for Halloween. How shall I save the seeds for next year's pumpkins? Oh dear, there are just too many, and I am so tired from working all this while."

"Sit down, Old Grandmother Pumpkin. You need to rest."

The children began to cover her with a blanket but she pushed it away. "No, no. There is no time to rest. The good gnomes are waiting. If only I had some help."

"We will help with whatever you need," the children cried out. "Now tell us!"

"Well," said Old Grandmother. "Each of you could care for one pumpkin. Carve it for Halloween. Save the seeds. Plant them when the gnomes say so in springtime. Then when Halloween comes again next year, please bring a pretty carved jack-o-lantern for me to see. It gets so dark in these woods this time of year. Oh how I do miss the Sun's spark.

"Oh dear, I must rest now. Please find the one pumpkin that sparkles just for you. Take it home, and thank you, my dear children. You have helped me so much."

The children began to cover Old Grandmother Pumpkin with the blanket. They tucked her into her rocking chair and tidied away her broom. Each child whispered a thank you. The children softly sang a lullaby for Old Grandmother Pumpkin. Then they went on their way, tiptoeing across the leafy forest floor, cradling their pumpkins full of seed babies. Quietly, quietly, humming all the way home . . .

Sing "Jack-o-Lantern" (American traditional song)

Jack-o-lantern, Jack-o-lantern,
You are such a funny sight
As you sit at my window
Looking out at the night

Once you were a yellow pumpkin
Growing on a sturdy vine
Now you are my Jack O'Lantern
Let the candlelight shine

The Animals Visit Mother Earth

DIANE VAN DOMMELEN

ALL SUMMER LONG, Little Bear had been growing and learning alongside his mother. But autumn was on its way, and the air was growing colder. The blueberries on Blueberry Hill were ripe, and Mother Bear began eating the berries all day long. Little Bear ate berries, too, but he still wanted to play and romp with his mother, as they had all summer.

"Not now, Little Bear," said his mother. "I must eat enough berries to keep us both warm all winter long in our den."

For a little while, Little Bear followed his mother and ate berries, too, but soon he forgot that mother bear was busy, and he jumped on her back!

"Oh, dear!" cried Mother Bear. "I do believe that you are ready to visit Mother Earth for the day, while I am busy doing my work."

And she led Little Bear down from Blueberry Hill and through the forest until they came to the cottage of Mother Earth. Mother Earth stood in her garden with a warm smile on her face.

"Mother Earth, could Little Bear stay here with you for the day?" asked Little Bear's mother.

"Of course," said Mother Earth. "I was expecting him."

So Little Bear hugged his mother, and she returned to Blueberry Hill, leaving Little Bear in Mother Earth's care.

Now, over in Sunny Meadow, Little Fawn and her mother had just tiptoed in from the tree under which they had been sleeping. Little Fawn smelled a new smell in the air.

"Fall is on its way," said Mother Deer. "Soon the leaves will dry up and the grass will be covered in snow. I must eat as much as I can now, before winter comes."

Little Fawn had been eating grass and corn from the farmer's fields all summer. Her legs had grown long and strong. She wanted to run and play, but Mother Deer was so busy!

"Little Fawn, let us visit Mother Earth. Perhaps it is time for you to make new friends to play with."

She led Little Fawn cautiously out of the Sunny Meadow and into the dark forest. Soon they arrived at Mother Earth's house.

"Mother Earth, could Little Fawn visit with you for the day? She is ready to make new friends."

Mother Earth smiled and opened the gate to the garden. Little Bear and Little Fawn looked at each other shyly for a moment before they began a game of chase! Mother Deer returned to Sunny Meadow.

High in the foothills of Rocky Mountain, Mother Coyote had just left her den. She put her nose in the air and smelled snow! If her cub was to stay warm this winter, she would have to go hunting today! But Little Coyote came bouncing out of the den into the sunshine! He was ready to wrestle.

"Not today," said his mother. "Today, I must find us some food. You are old enough to visit Mother Earth for the day and play there. You see, Mother Earth has been busy all summer and is ready for the long winter ahead. It warms her heart to have her little friends come and play in her garden."

Little Coyote was curious! "Let's go!" he said.

So Mother and Little Coyote ran down from their rocky den and straight through the forest. When they arrived, Mother Earth invited Little Coyote in for a warm snack and story. And Mother Coyote ran back to Rocky Mountain to hunt for food.

The little animals had a lovely time with Mother Earth. They played games. They painted and colored pictures. They ate a delicious snack. They sang songs and heard wonderful stories. They even snuggled with Mother Earth and rested a little, so they would be ready for the journeys back to their homes. At the end of the afternoon, the mothers returned from their busy days to gather their little ones.

"Please," cried Little Bear, Little Fawn, and Little Coyote all together. "Could we play again with Mother Earth tomorrow?"

"Of course," said their mothers.

And so it was.

Mouse Gets Ready for Winter

MEG FISHER

All summer long Little Mouse had a wonderful time. He woke to the warm morning sunlight, found plenty of food in the Farmer's corn field, and sometimes a treat under the farmhouse porch when one of the children would drop something.

He scampered everywhere, exploring the long, sunny day and at night when darkness came, he curled up happily and went to sleep, with a leaf for a blanket.

But one morning the air was chilly, and Little Mouse shivered as he slept under his leaf.

Then something hard and round fell out of the big oak tree. Plop! and woke him right up!

"What is happening?" he wondered.

"Woooo!" said the wind. "Autumn is here and Winter is coming. It is time for you to make yourself a mouse hole where you can stay warm."

Little Mouse looked all around until he found some soft earth between the roots of the old oak tree. He dug and he dug until he had made himself a fine mouse hole. And since the sun was going down, he brought his corn supper inside, ate it, and fell asleep.

The next morning the air was even chillier and, even though he was in his new mouse hole, Little Mouse shivered.

"Why am I still so cold?" he wondered.

"Woooo!" said the wind. "You need to line your mouse hole with soft, cozy things so that it will be warm even when the snow falls."

Little Mouse gathered red leaves for his bed. When he lay down in them, they rustled and crackled happily. They would keep him warm and dry. But his mouse hole was still not cozy enough. What else could he find to keep himself warm?

Off to the nearby farmhouse he scampered, to see what he could find.

On the farmhouse porch a little girl was brushing her hair.

> *"I'm brushing my hair, I'm brushing my hair,*
> *I'm brushing here, I'm brushing there,*
> *I'm brushing my hair."*

Little Mouse hid behind the haystack. When the little girl had finished brushing her hair, she cleaned the brush and lay the soft cloud of hair onto the ground for the birds, just as grandmother had taught her to do. Then she went inside.

"Oh how soft and oh how golden," sang the Little Mouse as he scampered back to the mouse hole with his prize.

When he returned, Grandma was on the porch knitting a scarf for the little girl to keep her warm.

> *"I'm knitting a scarf, I'm knitting a scarf.*
> *I'm knitting here, I'm knitting there,*
> *I'm knitting a scarf."*

When she got up to go inside and make supper, some scraps of yarn fell from her lap.

"Oh how soft and oh how blue," sang Little Mouse as he scampered back to the mouse hole with his prize.

When he returned, the sheep were just coming home from the pasture for their supper, and some of their wool got stuck on the old fence as they passed.

"Oh how soft and oh how white!" sang Little Mouse as he scampered back to his mouse hole with his prize, just as the sun was setting.

Then he pulled and he pushed and he poked until he had gotten everything just right and then he snuggled himself right in the middle of his soft, warm nest, ate several pieces of golden corn and closed his little eyes.

"Wooo!" said the wind. "I see you are all snug and warm there tonight."

"Yes," said Little Mouse, "I have lined my nest just in time!"

Plop! Plop! dropped the acorns.

"Woooo!" said the wind.

But Little Mouse was already fast asleep.

Little Apple Mouse

ANDREE WARD

Andree's "prop" for this story is a hollow, red felted apple with an adorable mouse inside. You will need something similar for the performance, and will also need enough star finger puppets for all the children as well as the storyteller.

PART ONE:

IT WAS A COLD AND FROSTY DAY. All the leaves had fallen from the trees, and an early snow covered the ground. The North wind was blowing. Out in Farmer Brown's apple orchard, the last apple was hanging on the tree. It was swinging in the wind, back and forth, back and forth. At last, that rosy red apple, way up in the tree, fell down to the ground. It rolled and it rolled and it rolled, round and round, until it finally settled among the roots of the old apple tree.

Now, hiding under the leaves in those roots was wee little Mousekin. She was beginning to shiver because it was so cold. She was the smallest member of the mouse family, but she was very brave and very strong. And it was time for her to find a cozy house for the winter. When the apple rolled right up next to her, she took a good look and thought to herself, "That nice red apple would make a fine meal, but it would make an even better house." So, she nibbled and she nibbled until she had made a little hole, just big enough for her to crawl inside. She was surprised to find something quite beautiful inside the apple. It was a star.

Sing to "My Nice Red Rosy Apple" or any simple mood-of-the-fifth tune:

> *My nice red rosy apple*
> *Has a secret from afar.*
> *If you could slip inside*
> *You'd see*
> *A lovely golden star.*

Mousekin hung her apple star way up in the tree. Next, she began to make her house comfortable and snug. She found some silky milkweed fluff under the leaves and took it into her house for a soft bed. Then she pushed all the leaves up snug around the apple.

"That looks like a warm and cozy mouse house, and it's just the right size for me!"

By this time evening had come, and many, many stars were sparkling up in the sky.

Encourage the children to "Let our little stars shine up in the sky."

Mousekin looked up at her own apple star in the tree and at all the stars in the heavens, and she was so happy. And the stars sang her a special night time song.

Sing to a traditional lullaby tune or any simple mood-of-the-fifth melody:

> *Lulla, lulla, bye, my baby close thine eye.*
> *With bells and flutes and lyres a-ringing,*
> *All the stars in Heaven are singing.*
> *Lulla, lulla, bye, my baby close thine eye.*

What a beautiful winter night! And little Mousekin snuggled into her warm little apple house, right into her own silky, fluffy bed. She was very tired from all her hard work, and she went right to sleep.

Sing the lullaby song.

PART TWO

To be told immediately after Part One or at a later time, depending on the age of the children.

THE NEXT DAY was just as cold and frosty as the day before, and Farmer Brown's young son, Jack, went down to the apple orchard to see what he could see. And he saw that the last apple had fallen from the old apple tree and rolled down under the roots. He crept closer, and he saw tiny Mousekin slipping out of her apple house.

"That's a fine little house for a very small mouse," he said to himself.

And then he watched as Mousekin began to scurry about, here and there, here and there.

"That wee Mousekin must be very cold and hungry."

Jack ran home and told Mother about Mousekin. who lived inside an apple out in the orchard. "Mother, she has found a nice winter home, but she has nothing to eat!"

Mother asked, "Jack, would you like to bring Mousekin some birdseed? Mousies love birdseed just as much as the birds do."

"Oh yes!" said Jack.

So Mother gave him a tiny bag of seeds for his tiny little friend. Jack took the seeds out to the orchard. Mousekin was nowhere in sight.

Could she be napping in her apple? Jack placed the little bag right next to Mousekin's apple. Then he hid himself to wait and see what he could see.

Jack was very quiet and still, just as quiet as a mouse. Sure enough, after a short time, a tiny nose poked out of the apple. Then, carefully, Mousekin crept out and saw the bag of seeds. She thought, "I wonder what friend brought me this lovely bag of seeds." And she pulled the bag inside her house.

Jack quietly and very happily went home to tell Mother. That night Mousekin sat on top of her apple house again, and over in Farmer Brown's house Jack looked out of the upstairs window. Mousiekin and Jack were both looking up at all the sparkling stars in the night sky. And the stars began to sing their night time song for Mousekin and for Jack.

Sing the lullaby song.

It was such a lovely lullaby that both Mousekin and Jack curled up in their beds and were soon fast asleep. And from that day right on through the whole winter, Jack brought little Mousekin seeds, and she was never hungry again. And every night, as Jack looked up at the bright winter stars, he thought about his little friend out in his father's orchard all snug in her cozy apple house. And little Mousekin looked up at the starry winter sky and thanked the sparkling stars for her new friend, who brought her seeds every day, and for their beautiful star music.

Sing the lullaby song.

RESOURCES

"My Nice Red Rosy Apple," Traditional German. See Jennifer Aulie and Margret Meyercort, editors, Autumn, *(Stourbridge, England: Wynstones Press 1999) p. 40.*

"Lullaby," Traditional German.

Stories for Winter Time

The Bear

STEPHEN SPITALNY

The winter now is cold and deep.
In his cave, the bear lies fast asleep.
His empty stomach rumbles and groans.
He wakes from sleep and stretches and yawns.
The hungry bear, no longer asleep,
Goes out looking for something to eat,
On front paws and hind feet.
He wants to eat and go back to sleep.
Here is a forest, tall trees all around,
The tree tops are far from the ground.
The trees of the forest stand side-by-side,
The branches stretch out far and wide.
The bear looks and what does he see?
Some leaves still cling near the top of one tree.
The bear climbs and climbs and climbs so high
Up and up and up to the sky.
Out on the branch he carefully creeps
He eats the leaves, they taste quite sweet.
Back he creeps, no more leaves around,
Down the trunk, down to the ground.
On front paws and hind feet,
The bear trudges through forest deep.
Now in his cave, he curls up tight,
Cozy he slumbers. Goodnight, goodnight.

The Child and Sister Star

AN ADVENT LEGEND ADAPTED BY LESLIE BURCHELL-FOX

LONG AGO AND FAR AWAY there lived a little child, a tiny child. The child lived with Father Sun under the great arch of the sky.

One morning the child asked Father Sun, "Where do I belong?"

And Father Sun answered, "I cannot tell you. You will have to go out and find your sister Star. She will certainly show you."

So the tiny child started on a long journey across Heaven, to ask his sister Star to show him where he belonged. Long he went and far he wandered until he came to the brightest star in Heaven.

"My beautiful sister Star," he said, "will you help me find where I belong?"

"Yes, brother child," she said. "You must follow me, and listen."

And off they went to find a home for the little child.

Long they went and far they wandered until they came to the Earth. Here the tiny child could neither walk nor even make a sound. Sister Star led him along until they came to the Crystal Mountain.

As her star-light fell on the crystals, they woke up and said, "Stand tall and walk, little child." And so he did. He walked on, following sister Star, and forgot all about the crystals on Crystal Mountain.

Long they walked and far they wandered until they found themselves in a garden. Right in the middle of the garden grew a Tree of Roses.

As sister Star's light shone on the roses, they woke up and said, "Breathe in and sing, little child." And he took a breath of their wonderful fragrance and exclaimed, "Ah!" He walked on singing and following his sister Star, and forgot all about the Tree of Roses.

Long they sang and far they wandered until they found themselves in a forest. There in front of them slept an Eagle, a Lion, and a Cow.

As sister Star's light shone upon them they woke and said, "Speak, little child, and give us our names." And for the first time the child spoke their names. He walked along following sister Star and called to all the birds and beasts of the forest, and soon forgot all about the Eagle, the Lion, and the Cow.

Sister Star was now getting a little ahead of the child, and he had to run to catch up. When he did, he saw that they were in the middle of a village, with many streets and many houses. Sister Star had come to rest above a small building and was shining in at the open door.

There inside, a mother and a father sat in the starlight.

"Who are you, little child?" asked the mother.

The tiny child looked up to the Star and remembered everything.

"I am yours," he said, "and here is where I belong."

A Baby Is Coming

AN ADVENT STORY BY JERRE WHITTLESEY

ONCE UPON A TIME, there was a donkey. This donkey was so sad, he hung his head.

A mother came to the donkey and said, "Donkey, why do you hang your head so low?"

"A baby is coming, a baby is coming, but I cannot find her!"

"Ah ha," said the mother, "soon you will see the baby."

There was also a sheep. This sheep was so sad, she hung her head.

The mother came to the sheep and said, "Sheep, why do you hang your head so low?"

"A baby is coming, a baby is coming, but I cannot find her!"

"Ah ha," said the mother, "soon you will see the baby."

There was also a mouse. This mouse was so sad, he hung his head.

The mother came to the mouse and said, "Mouse, why do you hang your head so low?"

"A baby is coming, a baby is coming, but I cannot find her!"

"Ah ha," said the mother, "soon you will see the baby."

Then one dark and starry night, the mother called the father, and the father called the donkey, and the donkey called the sheep, and the sheep called the mouse. When they were all together, the mother moved her blue mantle to the side, and there inside was a beautiful, new baby. The donkey, the sheep, and the mouse all began to sing their stable songs.

The donkey sang, "hee-haw,"
the sheep sang, "baa,"
the mouse sang, "squeak!"

And the angels in heaven joined their joyful song.

Sing to the tune of "Mary Sings Her Child to Sleep" or any simple tune:

Mother rocks her child to sleep
Mouse and donkey and the sheep
All are with her in the stall
And angels, angels, guard them all.

RESOURCES

Song lyrics adapted from Wilma Ellersiek, "Angels Guard the Child" in Nativity Plays for Children *(Edinburgh, United Kingdom: Floris Books 2014) p. 28.*

The Fiercest Little Animal in the Forest TERRI REINHART

THE PINE MARTEN was the fiercest little animal in the forest. When other animals came near him, he growled and snarled and snapped at them. Then the animals ran away. When people walked through the forest, he hid in bushes growling and snarling and snapping at them as they traveled by his bush. Then the people would walk a little faster to get away from the fierce little animal.

One day the pine marten heard people coming. There were lots of people marching straight through his forest! The pine marten hid in a bush by the path. As the people passed him, he began to growl and snarl and snap his teeth.

The people all rushed past the pine marten, except one man. He stopped and looked down at the fierce little animal. Suddenly, the pine marten did not feel so fierce. He tried to run away but was caught in the brambles of the bush.

The man bent down and gently picked up the pine marten and put him in his pocket. "I am Saint Nicholas and you, my little friend, are coming with me." The fierce little animal started to scrabble and scratch, but it was no use. He stayed in Saint Nicholas's pocket all the way across the forest. He stayed in Saint Nicholas's pocket when everyone boarded a ship and they sailed all the way across the sea.

When they finally arrived on the other shore, Saint Nicholas's helpers carried bags filled with flour, apples, nuts, and honey cakes. They traveled to a town where the people were very poor and very hungry. Saint Nicholas and his helpers left food on each and every doorstep.

Then Saint Nicholas took the pine marten out of his pocket and looked him squarely in the eye. "No more growling, no more snarling, and no more snapping. I have work for you to do," he said.

Saint Nicholas sent the pine marten into each house with a coin. Inside each house, he dropped the coin into a stocking that hung by the fire. He worked all night long.

When morning came and he was finished with his work, he was very tired. He was happy to go back inside Saint Nicholas's pocket. The little pine marten was so sleepy that he did not know when they boarded their ship and sailed across the sea for home. He did not even wake up when they arrived at his forest.

When they arrived at the pine marten's home, Saint Nicholas lifted him out of his pocket and put him down on the ground. "Your work is done now, my little friend. You can go free."

But the little pine marten wanted to stay with Saint Nicholas. From that time on, the pine marten lived in the woods close to Saint Nicholas's house. Whenever Saint Nicholas needed his help, he was always right there.

A Story Sequence for Early Winter ADAPTED BY SHARIFA OPPENHEIMER

Years ago, Sharifa attended a talk by respected storyteller Margret Meyerkort, who discussed her wintertime stories and described how each kingdom—mineral, plant, animal, and finally human—took a step in evolution as part of the Christmas miracle. These stories are inspired by that talk, and offered with gratitude for the foundations provided by Margret and other storytellers. Sharifa likes to tell these stories just before Christmas. They are stories of transformation, giving images to the young child of the forces of growth in the natural world as well as within the kingdom of humanity. The three stories can be told during three consecutive weeks. For the fourth week, these winter stories have set the stage for each family to tell their favorite seasonal story at this time of the Return of Light.

In the temperate-climate region of Sharifa's home, there are many winter stories that use the images of light being born out of darkness. She focuses on a tradition familiar to her culturally. Telling these stories is a way to focus on the deep spiritual significance of the cyclic transformation of light and its corollary importance in the human soul. The stories speak of the transformation of consciousness, beginning with the mineral kingdom in the crystalline formation of the snowflakes that are as lovely as roses. They move through the plant kingdom with the story of the little fig tree, and on to the animal kingdom in the story of the robin.

The final story may be chosen to tell about the transformation of our humanity, the story of the "child of light." In each story, we see the central figure take a step in evolution; we see something brand-new appear. Sharifa believes these stories are taken from an ancient medieval tradition. They are intended to delight and inspire.

THE FIRST WINTER ROSE

ONCE UPON A TIME, in the deep cold of winter, an old man and a young woman began a long journey. They packed their few belongings onto the back of a little gray donkey, and so they went along, up one hill and down the other. As they traveled, the winter wind began to blow. The young woman pulled her cloak more closely around her shoulders. She shivered. The day wore on and her footsteps became slow.

Finally, as they stopped to rest, the old man said to her, "Here, my dear, let me carry our bags, so the donkey can carry you."

Wearily, she climbed onto the donkey's back.

At last, as the sun moved toward the horizon, they saw the first lights of the evening twinkling in the town below.

"Soon we will be warm and well fed," said the old man. "I know of an inn just at the edge of town."

"Thank goodness," said the young woman, "for it has just begun to snow."

Snowflakes fell like silent diamonds as they hurried toward the lights. But when they arrived at the inn, they found all the rooms had been taken. There was no place for them to sleep.

"Never mind," said the old man. "Do not worry. There are other inns further ahead."

But at each inn they found the same thing: all the rooms were taken, and they had no place to sleep. At length, they came to the last inn.

"Surely here, there will be a place for us," the young woman whispered. "If not, what will we do?" A tear glistened on her cheek.

Alas, this inn also was full. Just as the inn-keeper began to turn them away, he saw the look in the young woman's eye and found himself telling these weary travelers they might stay overnight in his stable, out behind the inn. "My animals will keep you warm, and the stable boy will bring extra hay, that you may have a fresh bed."

Gratefully, they followed as he led them around the corner toward the back of the inn.

Inside the stable, the hay was golden and fragrant upon the earthen floor. The curious animals came close, their breath warm and sweet. The old man arranged her cloak upon the hay, and the young woman lay down.

Then, something wonderful happened! A baby was born to them that night. The man, the woman and all the gentle animals, gazed into his shining, brand new face. Soon, though, the baby grew cold, and although they wrapped him close and snug, he began to cry. The old man gathered a bit of hay, and a few twigs and sticks. He began to build a small fire to warm them all, for the cold had grown bitter. When the tiny fire burned bright, he put on his cloak, that he might go outside to gather some bigger branches.

Outside, he found the snow had fallen deep. Everything lay under a thick white blanket. He had to walk far, up to the top of a hill, to find a great old fir tree. There, under the fir, sheltered by its limbs, still green in the middle of the winter, he found dry sticks and large boughs, which he gathered in his arms. Slowly he made his way back toward the stable.

Once inside, he built the fire up again, placing the wood this way and that, till the flames danced merrily before them. The baby quieted down, no longer crying, now that he was warm. When he opened up his little eyes, he saw, on the old man's beard, a tiny snow drift glittering in the firelight.

Seeing the twinkling snow, the baby just laughed out loud for pure joy. When the snowflakes heard the baby's laughter, they became so happy that their sparkling little hearts burst into bloom! And there stood the old man, in the middle of winter, his beard full of tiny white roses!

Everyone was very happy, indeed.

THE FIG TREE

O NCE UPON A TIME, there was a little fig tree. She grew happily on a hill, close beside a stable. She loved her hillside, and all the busy goings-on at the stable close by. In the spring, she watched as the shepherd maiden brought the new lambs and their mothers out into the green meadow, to eat the soft spring grasses. In summertime, she saw the shepherd maiden bring the flock up higher on the hill, to catch the cool breezes. At autumn's harvest, she breathed the fragrant perfume of fresh-mown hay, as bales were stacked into the stable for the coming cold. In winter, she thrilled to the silent snow, shimmering under the light of the moon.

She knew everything there was to know about life on her hillside. And so, you can imagine how very surprised she was on the frosty winter night of which this story tells.

The shepherd maiden had brought fresh hay, the animals had been fed, and the stable door was locked, that the animals be snug for the night. All was as it should be. Until, surprisingly, the innkeeper led an old man, a young woman, and a little gray donkey out to the stable.

"What on earth is this?" the fig tree wondered to herself.

The innkeeper returned to the house, but the man and woman stayed inside the stable. Humans did not sleep in the stable for the night, except perhaps an occasional shepherd, on a warm summer's eve. Surely these people couldn't mean to sleep here! Humans had such thin skin, not properly thick and rough, like her excellent bark, or even sensibly furred, like her friends, the animals. How would they survive the cold? She wondered these things as she watched from her place close by.

Suddenly a brilliant light was kindled, right there inside her stable! This light began to pour out through all the cracks between the boards, reflecting off the glistening snow. What was happening in there? She became ever and ever more curious. Soon the stable door opened. The old man, wrapped tight against the cold, began searching on the ground for something. He made his way up the hillside, stopping finally to bend down again and again below a giant old fir tree. When he returned, the little fig tree saw his arms full of pine boughs. She knew he was bringing the wood back to the stable. She determined that this time when he opened the door, she would stretch out her neck and peek inside. She wanted to see what this was all about, and where that dazzling light came from!

But when he opened the door, stretch as hard as she might, she could not quite see inside. Now what would she do? She became more curious than ever. She just had to find out!

In the distance, she heard the tiny sound of flute music wafting over the frozen fields. Soon, she heard the happy voices of the neighboring shepherds, singing their rowdy evening songs. When she knew that they were coming toward the stable, she was thrilled! When they opened the door, all she needed to do was stretch a little farther, to see all of this wonderment in the night. She swayed a little in the breeze, waiting in anticipation.

Finally, they arrived all breathless, and scrambling along. When the door opened, she stretched her farthest, and even a little more . . . but still she could see nothing.

Then she did something that no other of all the green-growing-things in the world had ever done! She let go of all the stones and crystals, which she had held so tightly with her rooty toes. She pulled one brown and barky foot up above the earth, and then she pulled up the other. Step by step, roots and all, she walked to the stable door.

And can you imagine what she saw? She saw that all the glowing light came from the shining face of a tiny new baby. There, in the manger, lay a fresh sweet baby! She was so happy to see this child of light, that she gave him his first birthday present. She bowed low before him, and offered him all of her round ripe figs. Every one smiled at the baby, at the delicious present, and especially at the little fig tree. It was a very happy night indeed.

ROBIN'S FIRST CHRISTMAS

As you remember, once, a very long time ago, an old man and a young woman took a long icy winter's journey. Because there was no room at the inn, they slept at night in a humble stable, with the animals' sweet breath warming them and golden hay for a bed. A baby was born to them that night. Although the old man made a small fire to warm the baby, still, the infant was cold. At the baby's cry, the old man put on his cloak. He went out into the snowy night to gather more wood, that the fire might burn warmer, to comfort the baby's tears.

So, the young woman was left alone. She needed to rock her baby and keep him wrapped snug, but also to tend the tiny fire of straw and sticks, keeping it alive till the old man returned.

This was not easy for the young woman. She was quite cold herself. Every time she stood up to gather a few more sticks, the baby's wrappings loosened, and he cried more pitiably. Each time she sat holding and rocking her baby, the little flames burned low, threatening to go out altogether. Back and forth she went, working between the fire and her very cold little baby. She tried not to cry, knowing it would upset the baby even more to hear her tears. Yet her eyes glistened in the firelight.

Now, this stable was made in such a fashion that up above, in the rafters, there were snug places, out of the wind and weather. Here a flock of little brown birds nestled through the winter. The birds had been watching, with their bright and curious eyes, all the surprising events of the evening. They saw the young woman's plight, and chatted, in their chirping voices, together.

"That poor baby is so cold."

"Do you know, humans don't even get to have feathers when they are babies!"

"Why, in the great blue sky, not? It would help everything so much, don't you agree?"

Many little feathered heads bobbed up and down.

"Well, feathers would certainly help keep him warm, but he hasn't got any. So, maybe we can help in another way."

There was a flurry of wings and tiny birdcalls. Suddenly the young woman saw a wee brown wing swoop low over the fire. She saw one piece of straw drop from an orange beak onto the smoldering fire beside her. The flames licked up the hay, hungry for more. Straw by straw, the flock of birds gathered and fed the flames. The fire burned more steadily now, and the baby grew calmer.

One bird, in particular, loved the baby's dear smile, and wanted to stay close beside him. So, this special little brown bird made it his duty to stand near the fire. He flapped his feathered wings to fan the fire, till the old man might return. He was happy to just be near this tiny new human being.

At last, the door opened with a whoosh of snow and cold. The old man threw down a great bundle of pine boughs, and got to work quickly. When at last the fire was cheery, and the baby slept soundly, the young woman saw that one small bird was still standing on the stable floor closeby. She looked carefully at him, and then she saw something that touched her heart. He had stood close to the fire, fanning the flames for so long, that his little round tummy had been burned! Now, his tummy was red! She reached out her hand and touched him, and then all the hurt went away.

"Because you love my baby so much and stood so close to the fire, from now on you and all your children, and all your ever-ever-so-great grandchildren will have red breasts. And you will be the bird best-loved by children all over the world."

So the very first robin red-breast twittered happily, and merrily flew to his family in the rafters above.

And everyone was happy indeed.

RESOURCES

Margret Meyerkort, Winter *(Stourbridge, United Kingdom: Wynstones Press 1983).*

The Winter Spiral

PEGGY FINNEGAN

THERE ONCE WERE A BROTHER AND SISTER who lived in a village by the edge of a forest. The villagers got their wood and food from the forest, and the children loved to play there every day. In the spring, they looked for wildflowers. They collected berries in the summer, and mushrooms in the fall. In winter, they bundled up to play in the snow.

One fine winter day they went out tromping in the snow to their favorite tree, whose branches spread right to the ground, so that it made a secret place for them. They gave the trunk a big hello hug, and as their ears were pressed against the lovely bark, they thought they heard a voice that said, "Dear children, whose hearts are good and true, long ago, the people of your village made beautiful celebrations in our woods, and the Earth was gladdened. But now our hearts are sad, for the people have forgotten how to bring gifts of beauty to the world. Can you help us please?"

The boy and the girl gave their word that they would try.

At the dinner table that evening they told their mother and father what had happened. Mother shared a story that her great grandmother had told her of a celebration from when she was just a little girl.

In the darkest part of winter, the villagers went from spruce tree to spruce tree, asking for a bough. When they had collected a whole pile, they took them to the meadow in the middle of the forest and created a beautiful spiral together. A candle was placed on a stump in the center. In the evening, the villagers all returned, each with an unlit candle in hand. One by one, they walked the spiral path to the center, lit their candles, and as they slowly walked out, they placed their candles along the path. Then they all sang together with love and joy in their hearts, grateful for the gifts from the forest and grateful for each other.

When the children heard this, they knew what they must do. The next day, they gathered their friends and their sleds to collect spruce boughs, thanking each tree for its gift. They took them to the meadow and made a spiral. Mother and Father found candles, but there were not enough holders. Then Mother said, "We have a lot of apples. That could work!" And Father carved a candle holder out of each one.

That evening all the villagers bundled up warmly and carried their apple candles to the meadow. There was the beautiful spiral in the snow. Father lit the candle in the middle, and one by one they each walked the spiral path. The children were quiet, listening to the lovely music playing, as the dark spiral slowly became filled with light. Then the villagers sang a sweet song together, and quietly walked home, holding joy and beauty in their hearts. And the earth, the forest, all the creatures, and even the stars were filled with joy.

Juno and the Sun Maiden's Garden CARLENE MOGAVERO

A winter spiral story.

THE SUN MAIDEN was a beautiful woman who sailed across the sky in a golden boat. Her long fingers reached the earth and brought light and life to everything. The stones glistened, the plants grew green, the animals played, and so did the children.

There was a child named Juno who watched the sun every day. She got up early every morning to greet the sun as it rose above the hills, and she would watch the sunset until her mother called her home. She collected pretty stones. She planted flowers and watched them grow. She played with the neighborhood kitty who wandered around her yard. Sometimes she played with friends, and sometimes she played by herself in the sun.

But then, as Juno watched, little by little, the sun's light began to weaken and the Sun Maiden's boat began to sink lower in the sky. Her journey across the sky began to shorten. The flowers began to wither. The trees began to lose their leaves, and the wind blew cold. Juno began to fear that the Sun Maiden was ill and might never return.

One day the Sun Maiden went into a cave in a high hill and disappeared from the sky. The villagers in Juno's town were now also afraid, so they ceased their daily work and gathered outside of the cave to sing to the ailing sun. They did not know why she had hidden herself in the cave, but they dared not go in. For three day's length the sun remained in the cave. For three days length the people sang.

In the darkest depth of the darkest night, young Juno stepped away from her mother and walked into the cave. She had a question for the Sun Maiden. The cave was dark, but there was just enough glow that she could walk without fear. It was the most beautiful cave. The walls seemed to glisten with gold. Ferns and vines grew in this cave. And there were apple trees. She even thought she saw birds resting in the trees. The pathway curved in and in, turning until she could see the sun maiden resting in the middle of a beautiful garden in a bed of roses.

"Have no fear, dear child." The Sun Maiden said.

The girl was so filled with awe, she almost forgot to speak. "Sun maiden, are you ill?"

"Ill? No, I am weak, but not ill. I am praying and gaining my strength to rise in the sky again, to lengthen your daytime, and once again fill your world with warmth, so the fruits may grow and the animals may play."

"The people are worried, Sun Maiden. I am worried."

Sun Maiden smiled and said gently. "Dear child, let me give you a gift." She plucked an apple from the tree and placed it in Juno's hand. Then she placed her glowing finger on its stem, and from the apple a lit candle rose. "Take this and return to your own garden and remember me in times of darkness. Even the brightness must pray for God's strength."

When Juno came out of the mouth of the cave, all were amazed. The little girl was holding the glowing apple, and she herself seemed to glow with love and golden light. She told her people what she had seen inside the cave, the garden, the apples and roses and evergreen, the crystals that sparkled and shone like stars. Juno told the people that they should have no fear. The Sun Maiden would return to the sky and summer would again come.

OPTIONAL ENDING

This ending may be omitted, as the images of the story are strong enough to stand on their own; or included, as the teller deems best.

So now at the darkest time of the year, when the light seems to all but disappear, we build our own gardens with curving paths of pine boughs filled with sparkling crystals, shells, roses, and animals from farm, forest, jungle, air, and sea. In the very center, we place a light. Then we walk, one at a time, to the heart of the garden to light our apple candles. We turn and bring our candles out, placing each one carefully on a star along the path. And, when everyone has had their turn, the evergreen garden is so bright with light, that it almost feels like the sun is rising on a new day. Our hearts are full of love and our minds are full of wonder as we return home.

Sampo Brings Back the Sun

JAN PATTERSON AND WASHANTI:IO, ADAPTED FROM A STORY BY INGER LISE

Jan and Washant:io adapted this story for their community Advent festival at Rudolf Steiner Centre Toronto. The student teachers made it into a shadow puppet show, as this suited both the children and the seniors who attended, and the theme of light returning was universal. They made little white fleece birds on a branch to give to all the guests, who were thrilled.

Wahshanti:io then adapted the story into a fleece table-top puppet show for the mixed-age kindergarten. The children especially liked the animals and the drumming. They changed the animals to include the reindeer as this also worked well for Washant:io's indigenous culture, and also to give the reindeer a significance beyond being "Santa's helpers."

The song "Oh, Great Spirit" by Lura Schwarz-Smith works well with this story.

WAY UP IN THE ARCTIC NORTH, where the winters are dark and cold, snow falls thick and lays itself like a blanket over the land for months and months on end. But the stars glimmer and sparkle like snow crystals beneath our feet. There in the Laplands, long, long ago, there was a little boy by the name of Sampo. He lived in a tipi, together with his family.

One evening, as Sampo lay snug, wrapped in his furs and waiting for sleep to come, he watched the grown-ups as they sat talking by the flickering light of the fire. The flames cast long shadows on the wall. The voices came and went. He drowsily listened to the music of their words, until suddenly Sampo heard his father's voice rise.

"It's no use," said his father. "The Great Spirit of Winter has taken over the world, and we will never see the sun again. It has been dark and cold for so long now, and we are in a bad way. Winter may well last forever."

They sighed. Shaking their wise heads, they huddled closer to the fire for a bit more warmth.

Sampo felt his heart pounding. The sun never to come back? He crept out of his furs and made his way to the fire. He took courage and spoke: "I will go and speak to the Great Spirit of Winter!"

But the old ones laughed. "You are much too small! The Great One lives far away on the seventh mountain, Rastekais."

But Sampo was determined to go and find the Great Spirit of Winter.

The next night, when everyone had fallen asleep, he crept out of the tipi and set out on his journey. He walked and walked. Long had he walked when tiredness started to creep up his legs. It was still very far, and the night and the snow seemed endless. Suddenly, a large wolf appeared out of the snow, its great silver-white tail swishing in the air.

"Where are you going?" asked the wolf with gleaming eyes.

"I am going to find the Great Spirit of Winter and ask him to set the sun free. Winter has been here for far too long. My village is freezing cold. We can't remember what the sun looks like anymore."

"You are a brave lad," said the wolf. "Come, climb on my back and I will take you. This is the night that all animals gather at Rastekais, the seventh mountain, to meet with the Great Spirit of Winter."

Sampo thanked the wolf and climbed upon his back. He gripped the thick silver-white fur tightly as the wolf bounded away.

They traveled a great distance until they could see the Great Spirit of Winter on top of the mountain, surrounded by the animals. This was the only night of the year when peace reigned on earth and all animals became friends. They could speak and ask the Great Spirit of Winter anything they wished.

"You'd better hide," said the wolf. "The Great One does not like humans. Only animals are allowed here!"

And Sampo asked, "Then can you ask for the sun to come back again with all its warmth and light?"

"No. From now on, you're on your own." And the wolf bounded away.

Surrounding the Great Spirit of Winter were all the animals of the mountains, plains, and forests. From the smallest lemmings to the wandering moose and the big white bears, all were there. They sat in silence and awe before the Great Spirit. And when he finally spoke, his voice thundered and the ground trembled.

Sampo hid himself behind the bears and from this place he listened to all the animals as they put forth their wishes. Sampo was afraid, but he had come on a mission.

Finally, he gathered all his courage and stepped forward. "Oh, Great and Powerful Winter, please let the sun come out again. It is so cold and dark where we live. Can you bring back the sun?"

"Who has brought this human child here?" roared the Great Spirit of Winter. "How dare a human bring such a question to me. I am the most powerful here and I do not need the sun."

Suddenly there was a chirping and cheeping; it was a little bird.

"But we would also like to have the sun back," it said in its small, tiny voice.

And when the other songbirds heard this, they also found their voices and their courage, and together they cried and cheeped and chirped: "We all want the sun back or we will surely freeze to death."

A great silence descended on them all as they looked up to the fierce face of the Great Spirit of Winter. They hardly dared to breathe and nothing moved.

But the smallest animals daring to speak up gave the bigger animals the courage to speak out, too. They all wanted the sun back! And so it was that the Great Spirit of Winter gave in, and the first golden rays of the sun fell upon the mountain tops, announcing its return.

And the little bird chirped to Sampo, "You had better hurry home now, for when the sun comes out and the day starts, peace will be over."

"Thank you for all the help!"

Sampo turned homeward. He ran as fast as his legs could carry him, but it was far. He knew that he wouldn't make it home before the sun appeared over his village.

But then Greylegs appeared before him again.

"Come on then! Jump up on my back and I will take you home!"

Sampo was very happy, sitting on the wolf's back. Its fur was soft and warm, and it did not take long before they were back at his tipi where his mother and father were waiting for him. As they neared the village the first beams of sunlight touched the earth and the enchantment ended. Greylegs threw Sampo off at full speed and continued on his way.

"Thank you!" shouted Sampo as he lay there in a snowdrift.

When the villagers saw the rising sun, they understood what Sampo had done. His mother and father were glad and proud to have such a brave boy, who had dared to stand up to the Great Spirit of Winter.

And from that time on, whenever Sampo was frightened, he remembered the courage of the little bird and realized that no matter how small you are, you can still be mighty.

From that time forward, every spring, Sampo waited patiently for the birds to return as a sign that the sun will follow.

RESOURCES

Inger Lise Oelrich, "The Warmth of Being" in The New Story: Storytelling as a Pathway to Peace (Leicester, United Kingdom: Troubador Publishing 2014).

"Oh Great Spirit" by Lura Schwarz-Smith in Mary Thienes-Schünemann, Sing a Song of Seasons (Fairfax, California: Naturally You Can Sing 2005).

The Lamp Lighter

MARY KNIGHTON

Mary developed this story out of a desire to bring a story for Advent that was both reflective of the season and inclusive of diverse religions and beliefs.

LONG, LONG AGO IN A SMALL VILLAGE, there lived an old light keeper. Every day he cleaned and polished his lantern, so the light would shine brightly. He tended the flame carefully so it burned tall and strong. Whenever the villagers needed to light their own lanterns, they could always go to the light keeper to receive a new spark.

However, the light keeper was getting very old. It was harder and harder for him to keep the light shining brightly. He called for someone new to tend the light. But none of the new, young light keepers lasted long at the job. They did not want to sit and tend the light all night. They wanted to dance and play and eat and drink. And they sometimes left the lantern unattended. Slowly the lantern began to get dimmer and dimmer. Soot built up in the windows, and the flame burned low. It was harder and harder for the villagers to light their own lanterns from this dim light. The village grew darker and darker.

One evening in midwinter, a young girl from the countryside came into the village seeking a light for her lantern. But when she came to the light-keeper, the last tiny flame flickered, faltered, and died out.

The girl stood alone in the dark. "Where can I find a light?" she wondered.

The old, feeble light-keeper was sitting in the corner. He spoke. "Deep in the forest you will find the light. But you must walk carefully and listen closely. Only then will you find the way."

The girl thanked the old man and walked out towards the forest. She shivered as she stepped into the dense woods. It grew darker and darker, and she had to feel her way between the trees. Her foot hit something hard in the path. It was a big stone. She pushed and she rolled the stone to the side of the path.

"Thank you," said the stone. So many people have kicked me on their way, but no one has bothered to move me, to make it easier to pass."

Now, whenever a stone stood in the path, she gently moved it aside.

The girl continued on. After some time, she felt a small fir tree blocking her path. It had fallen over in the wind. She propped it back up and patted the earth down around its roots.

"Thank you," said the tree. "Now I can grow straight and tall."

On she went. She heard a slight whimpering sound below her. She knelt down and felt something soft and furry. It was a little squirrel with a hurt foot. Carefully, she wrapped a soft cloth around its foot.

"Thank you for your kindness," said the squirrel. "If you will put me into my hole, I'm sure my foot will be better soon."

She lifted the squirrel up into his hole in the tree and gave it a little nut she had in her pocket.

Now she was in the deepest, darkest part of the forest. She stopped to gather her courage. She did not know where she would find the light. Then she heard crying. She ventured forward and there on a stump sat a very young child.

"I've lost my way," cried the child, "and I'm so cold and hungry."

"Here, take my cloak." The girl wrapped her cloak around the small child. She reached into her pocket and took out a bit of bread and gave it to the child. "Sit on my lap and I'll keep you warm." She put the child on her lap and sat down to rest.

She closed her eyes for a moment and felt a warm light stream into her. When she opened her eyes, it didn't seem quite so dark anymore. She looked up into the sky and saw all the stars as they shone brightly in the night sky. She looked at the ground and the stones seemed to glow with a soft light. The leaves on the plants and trees shimmered and glistened. All around, in little holes and burrows, she saw the bright eyes of the night animals glowing.

Then she looked into her hand and she saw her lantern was burning brightly with a strong, tall flame. "Oh," she cried, "I can take you back to the village now."

She led the child by the hand. It was easy to see the path now. Her lantern shone brightly and all the stones glowed, leading the way.

Soon they were back in the village. She found the child's home. His parents rejoiced at the return of their son. Then, as she shared the light gathered on her journey, they rejoiced at the glow that began to shine from their own lantern. The young girl went from door to door and shared this light with everyone in the village. Soon the village began to glow again.

The young girl became the new light-keeper. She tended her flame with care, and she taught all those who came to her how to care for their lanterns so that the light would always shine brightly.

How Glooskap Found the Summer
A MI'KMAQ INDIAN LEGEND
ADAPTED BY SUSAN HOWARD

Susan has had an interest in place-based folklore and indigenous stories for more than fifty years, and this particular story from the Mi'kmaq culture was a favorite among her kindergarten children on the Northeast coast of the United States many years ago.

ONCE IN THE LONG-AGO TIME lived the people of the early morning sun. Glooskap was their lord and master. He was ever-kind to his people, and did many great deeds for them.

Once it grew very cold, snow and ice were everywhere, fires would not give enough warmth, and the corn would not grow. Glooskap went to the far north where all was ice and at last came to a wigwam in which there lived a great giant. He was Winter, and his icy breath had frozen all the land. Glooskap entered the wigwam and sat down. Then Winter gave him a pipe, and as Glooskap smoked, the giant told tales of the olden times when Winter reigned everywhere; when all the land was silent, white and beautiful. As he spoke, a charm fell upon Glooskap—the frost charm. And as the giant talked and talked, Glooscap fell asleep. He slept like a bear for six months. Then the charm fled, as Glooskap was stronger than the charm, and he awoke.

Soon after he awoke and began to return to his own country, Tatler the Loon, his talebearer, a wild bird who lived on the shores of the lakes, brought him strange news. He told of a country far off to the south where it was always warm because there lived a queen who could easily overcome the giant, Winter. So Glooskap, to save his people from winter's cold, decided to find the queen.

Far off to the seashore he went, and sang the magic song which the whales obey.

"Whale, whale, come to me,
Take me far out to sea."

Up came his old friend, Blub the Whale. She said to Glooskap, "You must shut your eyes tight while I carry you. To open them is dangerous, for if you open your eyes I am sure to go aground."

Glooskap climbed on her back and for many days the whale swam, and each day the water grew warmer and the air more balmy and sweet. Glooskap could smell fruits and flowers. Soon they found themselves in shallow waters, close to the shore. Glooskap opened his left eye and peeped. At once the whale stuck hard and fast on the beach but Glooskap, leaping from her head, walked ashore. With a mighty push, Glooskap sent her into the deep water and the whale sailed far out to sea.

Far inland strode Glooskap. At every step it grew warmer, and the flowers began to come up and talk with him. He came to where there were many fairies dancing in the forest. In the center of the group was one fairer than all the others; her long brown hair was crowned with flowers and her arms were filled with blossoms. She was Queen Summer.

Glooskap knew that at last he had found the queen, whose charms could melt Old Winter's heart and force him to leave. He caught Summer up and ran away with her, and left the fairies far behind.

And so at last, after a long, long journey he came to the lodge of Old Winter, but now he had Summer in his arms. Winter welcomed him, for he hoped to freeze Glooskap to sleep again.

But this time the Master did the talking. This time his charm was the stronger, and ere long the sweat ran down Winter's face. He knew that his power was gone and the charm of the frost was broken. His icy tent melted and the snow ran down the rivers, carrying away the dead leaves. Old Winter wept, seeing his power gone, and he went away. Queen Summer used her strange power and everything awoke. The grass grew and the fairies came out.

And so it was that Winter left the land and summer returned to Glooskap's country.

RESOURCES

Mary D. Hutchinson Hodgkins, editor, The Atlantic Treasury of Childhood Stories (*Boston: Atlantic Monthly Press 1924*).

Louhi, Witch of North Farm

A STORY FROM THE KALEVALA, RETOLD BY TONI DE GEREZ

IT WAS SNOWING on Copper Mountain. Louhi, The Witch of North Farm, stretched and scratched her back.

"My! My! What shall I do today?"

She sat down on her bony behind to think about it. It was day and time to make some witch plans.

She muttered and sputtered. She grumbled and rumbled.

"Shall I bake bread? I could make blueberry soup. I could go down and look at the boats. Shall I start some new knitting?"

But none of these plans suited her. They were too everyday. They were not good WITCH plans. Louhi felt like stirring up some sort of trouble. What good is a witch who is too good? Louhi scraped some frost off the window and looked out. It was snowing softly. The snow looked just right for skiing: not too wet, not too icy. Just enough crust for the skis to glide along smoothly.

So Louhi put on seven layers of clothes, all on top of her nightshirt. Then she pulled on her boots, which were stuffed with good sweet grass. Louhi took down her mittens, which had been drying by the hearth.

Her skis were waiting by the door. Louhi liked to ski. Of course, she could wish herself into a bird and fly. She could wish herself into a fish and swim. She could wish herself into a stone and roll down a hill. But she felt like skiing in the world so white, so white.

"Hei! Hei! I'm off!" she said to Nobody, or perhaps to Sit-Behind-the-Stove, the quiet one. "There must be some witch-witch-witchety things to do."

She glided smoothly over many meadows of dry heather and over many low bushes. Far away, far away from North Farm, across many lakes and rivers and hills. And then Louhi changed her mind. Up high into the air, into the sky, into the snowy clouds Louhi skied. "This is the real way to ski," said Louhi.

Suddenly Louhi stopped. She could hear music. She looked down. It must be Vainamoinen. Only Vainamoinen could make music like that.

Vainamoinen was known all over the world, in all Four Corners. He was the Great Singer. He was the Great Boat Maker. Why, if he felt like it, he could sing a boat together with only his magic words! And he was the Great Knower. He knew about everything, Over and Under and Up and Down.

Louhi skied down a cloud-hill and hid behind a chokecherry bush. There he was! Vainamoinen was sitting on a stone. His harp was laid out flat across his knees. He drew his fingers gently across the strings and the tones leaped into a melody.

Vainamoinen played. Never before had there been such sweetness of sound. Birds came flocking to his shoulders. Fish came to the lake shore among the reeds. The pine trees made merry. Some old tree stumps hopped about as though they were young again. All the animals in the forest picked up their ears and came running: the deer, the foxes, the wolves. The Seven Stars of the Great Bear came circling down from the sky.

Vainamoinen played on and on. Even the sun and the moon wanted to come close. The white moon stepped out of the sky and settled upon a birch bough. The yellow sun came to rest upon a pine branch.

The music was so sweet. Not a single leaf moved. Not a pine cone dropped. All was still except for Vainamoinen and his music.

Suddenly Louhi the Witch came out from behind the chokecherry bush. Louhi made a double somersault over the bush. And Louhi turned into an eagle. Then, screaming and shaking with mean laughter, Louhi flew to the top of the birch tree. Louhi stole the moon! Louhi flew to the pine tree. Louhi stole the sun!

Off she flew with the sun and the moon. Louhi flew back to her North Farm. Then what did Louhi do? Louhi hid the moon and the sun behind nine great locks, behind nine great doors in her storeroom in Copper Mountain. Then she turned another double somersault backwards—and there was Witch Louhi, the toothless one, except for one old back tooth.

Louhi pulled up her stockings. She said, "Now for a little bowl of porridge! Where is my dear little porridge spoon?" And the porridge spoon jumped onto the top of the table.

Now it was dark everywhere. The land was plunged into terrible darkness. The people and wood creatures could not find their way home. Darkness was everywhere, dark, dark darkness. The wind howled angrily through the cold dark sky. Nobody knew whether it was morning or evening. Musti, the black dog, rolled up into a black, shivering ball. Muurikki, the black and white cow bumped around in her shed. The black door did not know inside from outside. Black smoke rising from the roof-hole asked, "Shall I blow North or South? It is all the same, nothing but dark."

Something had to be done. Everybody had worry on their faces.

Vainamoinen went to find his friend Seppo, the smith. Seppo was a great smith. He had forged the Sampo, hadn't he, the magic chest? Surely he could make a silver moon. He could make a golden sun. And the earth would be happy again.

Seppo, the smith, worked hard. At last he forged a beautiful moon. He forged a beautiful golden sun. He climbed the pine tree and placed the new sun on a top branch. He climbed the birch tree and placed the new moon there.

Nothing happened. There was no light. Darkness still covered the earth with a heavy blanket.

Seppo became very angry. "I shall make an iron collar and nine terrible iron chains to wrap around the neck of a certain Witch!"

CLANG, CLANG was the noise in his forge as he made the nine terrible iron chains and the iron collar.

Vainamoinen, in the meanwhile, went off to Copper Mountain to try to find the moon and the sun. Vainamoinen crossed mountains and rivers. At last he was near Copper Mountain. Louhi's dogs barked and growled. Louhi listened through the moss between the logs and peeked through a hole in the wall. Louhi opened the door a crack. She screamed, "The sun and the moon are here! But they are mine forever. Go Away!" And she shook her Nameless Finger at him, the most powerful of all fingers!

Vainamoinen went back home sadly, across marshes and rivers. But Louhi was curious. What were they up to now, those two, Vainamoinen and Seppo?

"I'll just fly over and find out," said Louhi. She changed herself into a hawk. She flew from North Farm to Seppo's forge. She perched on top of Seppo's door and asked in a pretty little voice, "What are you making, Seppo?"

He stopped his pounding for a moment.

He said, "I am making an iron collar and nine terrible iron chains to wrap around the skinny neck of a certain Witch!"

"But why are you doing that?" asked Louhi in a soft, sweet, little voice. "And who is the Witch, if I may ask?"

"She is the Witch who stole our sun and who stole our moon."

And a big stone of fear dropped into the heart of Louhi. Quickly she flew back to her Copper Mountain, to her North Farm. She took her nine iron keys and opened the nine iron doors of her storeroom. There were the sun and the moon. They were sitting sadly side by side.

Louhi picked them up in her arms. She flew back high over the marshes and the sea. She placed the sun back in the pine tree. She placed the moon back in the birch tree.

With another of her somersault tricks Louhi became a dove. She flew to the top of the door of Seppo's forge.

"What do you wish, little dove?" asked Seppo.

"Just to tell you the moon and the sun are back. Look! Look!"

Now there would be time: Night time and Day time. There would be weather: winter with ice and snow and cold winds. Summer with bright-eyed flowers, birds and tall grasses. The sun and the moon are back. Look! Listen! Louhi has flown back to her home in the North Farm. And Vainamoinen is singing again.

RESOURCES

Toni de Gerez, illustrated by Barbara Cooney, Louhi of North Farm *(New York: Viking Kestrel 1987).*

Rosie's Adventure on the Icy Pond WENDY WEINRICH

On the pond, cold wind, ice, and snow
Grandfather Turtle sleeps down below
Squiggle Toes Squirrel sleeps high above
His nest is built with his family's love
Rosie, the deer, plays on the ice alone
Then follows the path that leads her home

ONCE UPON A TIME, there was a small pond at the edge of the forest. The North Wind blew cold across the ice. There were no living creatures in view, although Grandfather Turtle was sound asleep beneath the icy surface in his muddy bed. Squiggle Toes Squirrel was also in his bed high up in the treetops, in the nest he and his family had made before winter had come.

Rosie, a young deer, poked her head out from behind the trees and cautiously stepped into the clearing near the pond. She had been there before with her mother and two brothers, but never all alone. Rosie sniffed the air and smelled the wood smoke. She knew that she was too close to the human dwelling. She sniffed again and stood very, very still. She did not know that Grandfather Turtle was deep asleep under the icy pond. She did not know that little Squiggle Toes Squirrel was fast asleep high up in his nest in the treetops. She thought that she was all alone.

Earlier in the day Rosie had lost her way as she followed behind her family. Now they were nowhere to be seen. Rosie was beginning to be afraid. She looked up at the bluestone-ridged cliff and saw the sun glowing orange as it was going to sleep behind the mountaintop. She took a few steps closer to the pond with her soft nose down near the green moss. She nibbled a bit but wasn't very hungry. She was too lonely to be hungry.

Then she saw the beautiful ice paintings that lined the edge of the pond. She knew that the ice fairies had been at work here. As she got closer she saw the brown leaves that had become frozen on the surface of the ice. Very slowly Rosie took a step out onto the frozen pond, then another step and soon all four tiny deer hoofs were on the slick surface of the frozen pond.

WHEEEE!

All of a sudden Rosie was ice skating! She felt as if she were flying across the ice. She sailed along and did some fancy spins as her four tiny hoofs kept her balanced and moving smoothly across the pond. What fun!

At last she was quite out of breath and headed toward the shore. Just before she got there she tripped over a twig sticking out of the ice and tumbled head over all four hoofs and landed in a pile of snow. She wasn't hurt, so she stood up and shook herself off. As she gathered herself together she looked down and saw deer tracks in the moss and some piles of deer pellets that smelled like her mother. Rosie was so excited and happy after her time on the ice, and now to find tracks of her family. She knew that she would find them somehow.

She slowly began to follow the tracks, sniffing as she went. She saw the long, fingerlike roots of the tall birch trees; they seemed to be pointing the way for her. She kept going. Suddenly, Squiggle Toes Squirrel appeared right in front of her.

"Follow me", he said, as he scampered away through the bushes and up the side of a hill.

Rosie followed, moving quickly now so as not to lose sight of Squiggle Toes. She trotted along, trailing behind the scampering squirrel. It was beginning to snow and the twilight seemed to brighten with the falling snowflakes. Rosie began to recognize the path. As she went further, she could no longer smell the wood smoke from the human dwelling. She knew that she was almost home. Squiggle Toes ducked under a bough from a cedar tree and Rosie followed. There she saw what she had been searching for.

She saw her mother and two brothers all huddled together keeping warm. They had found shelter from the heavily falling snow under a lean-to that the human children had made. It was the perfect size for a family of deer. The steep sides of the A-frame came all the way to the ground and the branches and boughs of pine that were piled across the frame kept out the wind and snow. Rosie ran to her family and was quickly nuzzling into the circle of warm bodies. Mother, brothers, and Rosie all lay down together in a circle, heads resting on one another's backs.

Quietly the snow fell, and a thick white blanket covered the roof of the lean-to. Rosie looked into her mother's warm brown eyes and sighed a deep sigh. She had found her family and she was safe and warm. She was home with the ones that she loved most. She closed her eyes and went to sleep. Perhaps she was dreaming of ice skating.

On the pond, cold wind, ice, and snow
Grandfather Turtle sleeps down below
Squiggle Toes Squirrel sleeps high above
His nest is built with his family's love
Rosie, the deer, plays on the ice alone
Then follows the path that leads her home

The Silver Pine Cones

A GERMAN FOLKTALE ADAPTED BY JENNY TAYLOR

This story has been only slightly adapted from the original to accommodate any storytime during winter season, without making reference to Christmas. It works well with puppets or for pretending with simple costumes.

IN THE BLACK FOREST OF GERMANY, there once lived a mother and a father and seven children. It was hard to find food enough for seven children. The family was poor, but they survived.

Then one year, in the coldest part of winter, the father fell ill. He could not go into the forest to hunt, so the family had no meat. He could not go into the forest to cut trees. Soon the family had no wood left for a fire.

One dark evening, the children sat cold and hungry. The father lay in bed, quite sick.

"I will go into the forest to collect pine cones," said the mother. "Then at least we will have a warm fire. And the sweet scent of burning pine cones may cheer us."

The woman took her basket and entered the dark forest, but she found no pine cones. Deeper and deeper into the forest she wandered.

Suddenly, she came into a grove surrounded by tall pines. Overjoyed, she began to gather up handfuls of pine cones from the forest floor. But as soon as the first pine cone hit the bottom of her basket a fierce voice spoke out!

By my boots and by my beard!
Who's stealing my pine cones?

"It's just me," gasped the frightened woman.

There behind her stood a dwarf. He was short but very stout. On his feet he wore big black boots. On his face he wore a long grey beard and a terrible scowl.

By my boots and by my beard!
Why are you stealing my pine cones?

"My husband is sick and cannot cut wood. My children are cold and hungry. I was gathering pine cones to make a fire this cold, dark night. I didn't know they were yours."

By my boots and by my beard!
Put those pine cones back!

The woman put the pine cones back where she had found them. She picked up her basket and started to leave. The dwarf stroked his beard and scowled.

By my boots and by my beard!
You'll find more down that path!

"Oh, thank you!" The woman hurried down the path in the direction he had pointed. Sure enough, there was another grove of pines. The woman stopped to gather a handful of the pine cones. She tossed them into her basket.

But as soon as the first pine cone hit the bottom of her basket, pine cones began to pelt down from the trees! From all around they rained down. Pine cones fell on the woman's head. Pine cones fell into her basket. Pine cones fell until they covered the ground. And still they did not stop.

"Bewitched! Bewitched! This place is bewitched!" she cried.

The woman grabbed her basket and ran from the magic pine grove. Behind her she heard a fierce voice boom out:

By my boots and by my beard!
That ought to be enough pine cones!

The woman ran for home as if a whole forest of dwarves were after her. As she got closer to home, the basket seemed to become heavier and heavier. By the time she had reached her little cabin she could barely carry it. She pushed open the cabin door and fell inside. Her basket dropped to the floor and turned over. Pine cones rolled across the floor.

The children sprang up crying, "Oh, Mama!"

For the pine cones which were rolling across the floor were not ordinary pine cones. . . They were cones of solid silver!

"It's enchantment! Wicked enchantment!" cried the mother.

"Wait a moment," said the father. "Tell me about what happened."

So the mother told about the dwarf and the forest which had pelted her with pine cones.

"This is not bad magic," said the father. "This is good magic. That dwarf you met in the forest must have been King Laurin, the Dwarf King himself! He is known to be very grumpy. But he is also known to have a kind heart where poor people are concerned. He has tried to help us! You must take some of these silver pine cones to town and sell them. You will be able to buy food and wood! Our fortune has changed!"

So the mother went to town with three silver pine cones. And when she had sold them there was enough money to buy food and wood and new warm clothes for the children besides!

What a feast they had that day!

But the father still lay ill in bed.

After dinner was done, the mother took raisins and spices and made a cake. She iced it prettily, wrapped it, and placed it in her basket. Then she set off for the forest once more.

When she reached the pine grove of the Dwarf King Laurin, the mother set the cake gently on the ground and started to leave. A fierce voice boomed after her:

By my boots and by my beard!
What's the meaning of this?

"It's a gift," said the woman. "I wanted to thank you."

The dwarf king grumbled and stroked his beard.

By my boots and by my beard!
Then I will give YOU a gift!

The Dwarf King leaned over and scraped away the snow from the ground. He picked a small herb that was growing there beneath the snow and handed it to the woman.

By my boots and by my beard!
Make tea for your sick husband!

The woman took the herb and hurried from the forest. She put the herb in a pot of water. She boiled it and made tea. But when the tea was done the water was a bright green!

"Husband," she said. "This is bad magic. Maybe the Dwarf King sent you poison."

"Would the Dwarf King send silver yesterday and poison today?" said her husband. "Give it to me. I will drink it."

And the husband drank down all of that green tea. As soon as he had swallowed the tea, his health returned. The strength returned to his arms. His head cleared. He was as well as ever.

From that day on things went well for this family. The children grew and prospered. They worked hard and earned their daily bread. But once in a while, when something special was needed, the mother would go to town to sell a silver pine cone. Much joy came of this.

But not all of the pine cones were sold. One silver pine cone was given to each child for a keepsake.

RESOURCES

Margaret Reed MacDonald, Celebrate the World: Twenty Tellable Folk Tales for Multicultural Festivals *(Hackensack, New Jersey: H.W. Wilson and Company, 1994).*

The Giant and the Gnome's Gifts LISE STOESSEL

ONCE UPON A TIME, there was a giant who lived way up high in the mountains. It was very cold all the winter long in his mountain home, and he did everything he could to keep warm. He had been having quite a problem with his toes, until a kindly gnome gave him two pretty bits of sheep's wool to wrap them up and keep them warm. It was a thoughtful gift.

One day, the giant went for a walk in the mountains, and on his way home the giant thought about what he could do to repay the gnome's kindness. Along the way, he passed a flock of sheep grazing in the meadow. The giant sat down on a big rock and watched the sheep as they slowly munched the grass and the weeds that grew in the rocky soil.

After a while, the giant noticed that there was a little bird flying back and forth between the meadow and a nearby tree. Soon the giant realized that the bird was gathering little bits of fluffy wool that had fallen from the sheep's coats. She picked them up with her pointy beak and flew back to the branches of a tree. The giant slowly and quietly crept a little closer, and he could see that the bird was making a warm nest with twigs and bits of wool. "How nice," the giant thought. "The sheep's wool is warming my toes and now it's making a nest for the bird and her family." Then he had an idea. "Maybe I could make a gift for the gnome with some of the sheep's wool!" That was a splendid idea.

So the giant gathered many little bits of wool that were lying among the rocks of the pasture and he stuffed them into his tall hat (for he had no pockets). As the day grew colder and the evening came, the giant climbed back up the mountain and finally reached his home.

It had been a long day and his tummy rumbled and grumbled, so he decided to make himself some supper. He looked in his cupboard to see what there was to cook. He found some onions, so he decided to make some soup. He got a big pot and put it on the fire and filled it with water from the stream. When the water was hot he added the onions with the skins on them, because they made such a beautifully colored broth. He stirred and he stirred his pot on the fire, and soon he began to feel a little bit hot. So he took off his tall hat, and down came tumbling some of the wool he had gathered and it fell—plop!—right into the pot. It took the giant a minute or two to find the wool, stirring this way and that, and finally he got it out. He hung it to dry over the fire, and he saw that the wool had turned a beautiful golden color! "Well," he thought, "that will make a fine gift for the gnome."

Now the giant thought about the other food he had on hand and he remembered some blackberries he had gathered last summer. They weren't actually in his cupboard; they were in his icebox, which was a little cranny in the side of the mountain just outside the door. It was a hole in the rocks that stayed cold all winter with the ice and the snow. He brought the blackberries in and sat them in a bowl to warm up. When the berries were warm they made a lovely purple juice and the giant thought, "Maybe I can put some of my wool in here and make it more beautiful for my friend the gnome." And so he did. He hung that wool next the other wool.

By now the giant was yawning; it had been a long day! He ate up his dinner and put on his jammies and jumped into bed. He had a very big bed. It was giant-size.

The next morning the giant took the pretty bits of wool, stuffed them into his tall hat and set off to find the gnome. His path crossed over a stream with stepping-stones. It was a cold morning and the stones were slippery, so he had to be careful as he stepped across. His arms waved this way ad that in the air as his feet slipped and slid on the stones. All at once he lost his balance and knocked his hat off of his head. As it went falling toward the stream he caught it in mid-air, but not in time to save the pretty bits of wool from falling into the stream. "Drippy wool does not make a very nice gift," he thought to himself, so he gathered it up and rolled and squeezed it in his hands until it was dry.

The funny thing was that with all that squeezing and rubbing, the bits of colored wool had formed themselves into a lovely little cloak, just the right size for his friend. "Well," he thought, "this might not be such a bad gift after all!"

And who do you think he met just then, on the path? It was the gnome!

"Hello," called a little voice. "And how are your toes today?"

The giant replied, "Very well, thanks to you. I was just on my way to bring you a gift."

"How nice," replied the gnome. "Won't you join me for tea?"

"I'd be delighted," answered the giant.

And so off they went to the gnome's house in the mountains. The gnome lived in a cave with a very tall ceiling, and it was a good thing, for the giant was a tall fellow. They had a lovely tea together. The gnome had made tarts and sliced apples, and they had quite a feast. The giant gave the gnome the beautiful wool cloak he had made and they both said to each other, "Isn't it wonderful to have such good friends?" And so it was. And they lived happily ever after.

Aloysius, the Keeper of Wishes

ANDREA LEE PISACANO

ON A COLD AND BLUSTERY WINTER AFTERNOON, two children overheard their parents talking in the kitchen of their tiny hut.

"If we do not sell the cord of firewood soon, we shall have no money for food for the children or ourselves," said the father sadly.

"Maybe the children are old enough now to forage for sweet yams and roots," said their mother.

The children looked at each other with worry. Suddenly the little boy's stomach made a great growl—*MRUMMNGH.*

The children went to their sad parents.

"Well," said the little girl, "we can go right now and forage for roots and yams before it gets dark."

"Be back soon and stay close to home!" said the parents. And they went back to cutting wood.

The children ran off and were soon skipping down a wooded trail into the forest. The sun was low in the sky behind the violet mountains, and patches of pink filled the trees. It was not long before they spotted the dusty green, pointed leaves of the wild yam. They dug their fingers eagerly into the soft earth. Filling their pockets, they started home, when the sky suddenly went very dark.

The tiniest specks of starlight began to appear through the treetops. There was a special quiet that seemed to be all around the children. Before they could become scared, the little girl hugged her small brother and began to sing her favorite bedtime song. The two huddled together and she sang:

All night, all day,
Angels watching over me, my Lord.
All night, all day,
Angels watching over me.

As she sang, a warm breeze, like a soft blanket, wrapped around the children and they were carried to dreamland.

Sing "Awake! Awake!" or any appropriate "wake up" song:

Awake! Awake! The Sun shines bright!

"Are we home yet, sister? I am so hungry," said the little boy to his sister. Rubbing her sleepy eyes, the sister again heard the loud rumbling from her brother's stomach—*HRUMMMGM.*

"Here, brother, look! There are pine needles to chew on, all full of good things and not a bad taste!"

The children chewed for awhile and then looked at each other. Holding hands, they looked for the trail back home. But first, they made a wish.

The two children spoke clearly and both wished from their heart of hearts, "If only we could find some real treasure, then we could help our parents. We wish, we really wish, for a way to find treasure."

Just then, from what seemed like out of thin air, a tiny house appeared in the clearing ahead. Out of the house came a small boy, nearly the same age as the children themselves. He was wearing finely tailored knickers made of soft blue velour, with a brown woolen jacket and a plush orange hat that had a spotted feather in it. He was holding a small lantern with a lit flame and he began to walk towards the children.

The children were curious, and shyly asked, "Who are you?"

Bowing deeply, he spoke softly and kindly, "Why, I am Aloysius, the Keeper of Wishes. I am here at your request. You children made a heart-felt wish, not a selfish one, but a wish to help your parents, and it is my duty to try to help you."

"Do you know how we can find treasure, then?" asked the sister.

"Well, today is the day that the fairies make their flower dust gold; we shall see if you follow me," said Aloysius.

"How do you know when the fairies make gold?" asked the little boy.

"It is the early morning pure winter light, see?" He pointed to a patch of shimmering sunlight on the dew. "Come and look!"

But all that the children could see was the sunlight.

In front of the children stood an ancient tree, as round about as their own hut. Aloysius knocked three times on the tree, and a small voice called out, "Who goes there?"

"It is I, Aloysius, the Keeper of Wishes."

Then a door opened into the tree to reveal two very small gnomes.

They said:

"We are so busy, as busy as can be,
But come join us for a cup of warm tea!"

The two kind gnomes led Aloysius and the children to a tiny table covered with a cloth and tiny tea set, with cups of tea for them all. As the children sipped the tea they noticed a staircase that seemed to be lit up from within the earth below. They heard something like music coming from there.

Aloysius and the children thanked the gnomes for the tea and were soon off down the staircase. As the children walked carefully in the darkness, they could not help but notice tiny shining crystals that reflected the lantern's light.

They heard gnomes chanting:

We gnomes are working in our den, in our den,
Through earth and rock below,
We tap, tap, tap, and then we dig
To find our precious stones.
We tap, tap, tap and rub, rub, rub
Until they gleam and glow.

The happy work song of the gnomes made the children eager to see more of them.

Down the stairs they walked until they saw a bright beam of light. Then, at the end of the staircase was a gleaming pile of glittering gems. The children's eyes were bedazzled. They pointed at the pile, speechless, and Aloysius said kindly, "Have patience, we are almost at the end of our journey."

The soft sound of tinkling bells seemed to come from farther ahead, and on they walked. Then suddenly they were in a small clearing, a sunlit meadow filled with tiny flowers. Aloysius crouched down to the ground and made a quiet sign to the children. Before their eyes, tiny specks of dancing light filled the meadow. Fairies!

Fairies flitted from flower to flower, each holding small bags and tiny wands. Tinkling bells played as they filled the bags with sunlight that had turned to golden dust.

"Oh, how I wish we could bring some fairies' gold to our home," said the little girl with all her heart.

At that moment, seven fairies flew right over to the children and each gave them their collected golden dust. The fairies were beautiful, each a color of the rainbow: red, orange, yellow, green, blue, violet, and indigo. In an instant they were gone, even before the children could say thank you.

The little boy, finding his words, sang out, "Thank you, thank you for your gifts, tiny fairy folk. Thank you for giving us a chance to bring this treasure to our home."

Aloysius smiled at the brother and sister and said:

"Whenever a heart-felt wish is spoken,
I do my best to see that it is not broken."

With that, he took the children's hands and they spun around in a circle three times and stopped.

Aloysius was gone!

The children felt the bags of treasure in their hands and felt their pockets still full of wild yams. They were facing their tiny hut, and their mother and father were stacking up the firewood with starlight overhead. The parents rejoiced to see the children again, with full pockets, and when they saw the golden dust they were amazed. And from that day forth, they always had enough to eat and enough to keep themselves warm.

RESOURCES

"All Night, All Day," American traditional. See, e.g., Marlys Swinger, editor, Sing Through the Day *(Farmington, Pennsylvania: The Plough Publishing House 1999) p. 105; The Metropolitan Museum of Art, Lullabies: An Illustrated Songbook (New York: Gulliver Books 1997) p. 91.*

"Awake! Awake!" Author unknown. This is a variation on a familiar verse in the Waldorf early childhood classroom, passed from teacher to teacher, and can be sung according to the storyteller's experience and inspiration. See, e.g., Ruth Ker, Please, Can We Play Games? *(Chestnut Ridge, New York: Waldorf Early Childhood Association of North America 2018) p. 97.*

Except as noted, the little songs in this story are Joani's original words. She performs them accompanied by pentatonic tunes, and encourages storytellers to make up their own tunes.

Mr. Snowman's Search

JOANI LACKIE-CALLIGHAN, ADAPTED FROM A STORY BY GERDA MARIE SCHIEDL

Sing an opening song:

> *Oh where do you come from, you little flakes of snow?*
> *Falling, falling, gently falling, to the earth below.*
> *On the trees and on the bushes and the mountains afar,*
> *Oh, tell me, do you come from where the angels are?*

FAR UP IN THE HEAVENLY SKIES, the snowflakes heard the stars talking about the wonderful colors found on the earth. All the colors of the rainbow could be found among the flowers living in the valleys, fields and woodlands.

Oh, how the snowflakes wanted to see what it was the stars were talking about, so they decided to fall to earth.

> *Snowflakes so light, snowflakes so white,*
> *Cover the earth and make it white.*

The snowflakes fell and fell all night, making the fields all white. They gathered together and formed a snowman. He had a long carrot nose, two coal eyes, and a warm woolen hat and scarf. But he was not a happy snowman; in fact, he was quite disappointed. For everywhere he turned his coal black eyes, all he could see was white.

He thought and thought and finally decided that he must be in the wrong place to see the colors of the rainbow.

"I know," he said aloud, "I'm just in the wrong spot!"

So he went venturing, and on his way to look for flowers the colors of the rainbow, he sang to himself:

> *Slipping, sliding, on my way.*
> *Looking for the flowers gay.*

It wasn't long before he came upon a little bunny munching on a cabbage. The snowman looked at the bunny and pointed to the cabbage saying, "Is that a flower?"

"No, silly snowman," the bunny replied, "it's a cabbage."

"Then could you please point me in the direction of the nearest flower?"

The bunny looked at the snowman and sadly sang,

> *Little snowman, it's sad I know,*
> *But since you live in a world of snow,*
> *You'll never see the flowers grow.*

"No, you're wrong," said the snowman. "I'm just in the wrong place, and you must be too. I'll be on my way."

The snowman departed singing,

Slipping, sliding, on my way.
Looking for the flowers gay.

His travels brought him to a small forest where he found a cardinal sitting atop an evergreen tree. The snowman had never seen anything so tall and green.

"Is that a flower?" he asked the cardinal.

"No, you silly snowman," replied the red bird. "This is an evergreen tree."

"Well, I am on my way to find flowers all the colors of the rainbow."

The cardinal looked into the snowman's coal dark eyes and sang,

Little snowman, it's sad I know,
But since you live in a world of snow,
You'll never see the flowers grow.

"No, you must be wrong," the snowman responded. "I will find flowers, and when I do, they will be all the colors of the rainbow. They're just not here, that's all."

And on he walked.

Slipping, sliding, on my way.
Looking for the flowers gay.

Coming out of the forest, he found a mouse nibbling on a pumpkin. He pointed to the pumpkin and asked the mouse, "Is that a flower, it's so beautiful!"

"No, Mr. Snowman, this is a pumpkin. Haven't you ever seen a pumpkin before, you silly snowman?"

"I wish everyone would stop calling me silly. I'm not silly, I just want to see some flowers, all the colors of the rainbow!"

The mouse sadly sang,

Little snowman, it's sad I know,
But since you live in a world of snow,
You'll never see the flowers grow.

The snowman began to cry. As he cried, his tears began to melt his face. The mouse was very concerned.

"Wait, Mr. Snowman, don't cry! I will help you find the flowers."

"You will?" the snowman asked.

"Yes, yes, I think I know someone who could help you. At the edge of the forest field you will find a little house. Magical things happen there. If there was ever a place to find your heart's desire, it is there."

"Thank you, thank you," replied the snowman, and he was on his way.

Slipping, sliding, on my way.
Looking for the flowers gay.

As he approached the house, a beautiful woman dressed in white with a royal cape and crown of fur came to meet him.

"Hello Little Snowman, I'm Lady Winter, and I have heard your heart's desire in the wind."

Snowman excitedly replied, "Then you know I'm searching for flowers all the colors of the rainbow?"

"Yes, dear one."

"Can you help me?"

"Well," said Lady Winter, "it just so happens that when Mother Earth called all of her Flower Children to nap underground with her for the winter, several children did not listen. I rescued them from King Winter's cold and they are spending the winter inside with me. But, alas, they cannot come outside, and you, my friend, cannot go inside, without causing great harm to yourself."

"Please, Lady Winter, I want to see the colors of the rainbow. I have come so far."

"Dear Mr. Snowman, if you will come with me, I will take you around to the back of my home, where through the windows you may be able to see my Flower Children friends inside."

So as Lady Winter guided the Snowman to her backyard, he peeked into the windows, and what do you think he saw?

A lovely rainbow of colors spread . . .
Pretty flowers from toes to head.

Mr. Snowman's heart was so warmed by the sight, he thought he might melt from the inside out, but he did not. In fact, he stood guard all winter in Lady Winter's backyard and was able to gaze at the lovely colors anytime he pleased . . . all the colors of the rainbow.

RESOURCES

Gerda Marie Scheidl and Jozef Wilkon, Flowers for the Snowman *(New York: NorthSouth Books 1998).*

"Oh Where Do You Come From," German traditional nursery tune. See, e.g., Jennifer Aulie and Margret Meyerkort, Winter *(Stourbridge, United Kingdom: Wynstones Press 1983).*

Wee Robin's Valentine Song

ADAPTED BY SHARIFA OPPENHEIMER FROM A STORY BY OLIVE BEAUPRE MILLER

ONCE UPON A TIME, an old gray Pussycat went out for a walk, pit-pat, on a bright and snowy morning. As she was walking along, there in a bush she saw a wee, wee Robin Redbreast hopping about on a branch.

"Good morning, wee Robin," said she. "Where are you going on this cold and frosty morning?"

"I'm going to see the King," answered Robin. "I'm going to sing a song for him to tell him spring is coming soon."

"Oh, but wait, before you go," said the Pussy. "Just hop down to me a minute and I'll show you a bonny white ring that I have around my neck."

But Robin looked down on Pussy with a twinkle in his eye. "Ha! Ha! old gray Pussy," said he, "you may show your white ring to the little timid mouse, but I'll not wait to let you show it to me! I'll fly straight on to the King!"

So he spread his wings and flew away. And he flew, and he flew, and he flew, till he came to a fence where sat a greedy old Hawk who was looking about for breakfast.

"Good morning, wee Robin," cried the greedy old Hawk, "where are you going on this cold and frosty morning?"

"I'm going to see the King," answered Robin. "I'm going to sing him a song to tell him spring is coming soon."

"Oh, but wait,before you go," said the greedy old Hawk, "and I will show you a bright green feather I have in my wing."

But the wee Robin did not like the look in the eye of the greedy old Hawk. "Ha! Ha! old Hawk," said he. "I saw you peck at the tiny birds, but I'll not wait to let you peck at me. I'll fly straight on to the King!"

So he spread his wings and flew away. He flew, and he flew, and he flew, till he came to a hillside where he saw a sly red Fox looking out of his hole.

"Good morning, wee Robin," said the sly old Fox. "Where are you going on this cold and frosty morning?"

"I'm going to see the King," answered the wee Robin. "I'm going to sing him a song to tell him spring is coming soon."

"Oh, but wait, before you go," said the sly old Fox, "and let me show you a queer black spot I have on the end of my tail."

"Ha! Ha! sly Fox," said the Robin. "I saw you chase the little lambie, and I'll not wait to see the spot on your tail. I'll fly straight on to the King."

So the Robin flew away once more, and never rested till he came to a rosy-cheeked boy, who sat on a log and ate a big piece of bread and butter. Then he perched on a branch and watched him.

"Good morning, wee Robin," said the boy. "Where are you going on this cold and frosty morning?"

"I'm going to see the King," answered the wee Robin. "I'm going to sing him a song to tell him spring is coming soon."

"Come a bit nearer," said the boy, "and I'll give you some crumbs from my bread."

"No, no, my little man," chirped the Robin. "I saw you catch the goldfinch, and I'll not wait for your crumbs. I'll fly straight on to the King."

So, no matter who begged him to stop and wait, the wee Robin flew straight on to the King.

He flew to the windowsill of the palace. There he sat and sang the sweetest song he knew. He sang because his heart was full of joy. He sang because spring was coming soon. He sang, and he sang, and he sang.

The King and Queen sat listening at the window. They were so pleased with his cheery song that they asked each other what they could do to thank him for his loving thought in coming so far to greet them.

Just then Jenny Wren, who lived in a golden cage in the castle, began to hop up and down and flap her wings. The Queen opened her cage door and Jenny flew out of the cage, out of the window, and sat happily singing by Robin's side. They sang and they sang. They sang because their hearts were full of joy. They sang because spring was coming soon.

It wasn't long before Robin Redbreast and Jenny Wren were married. And so they, the King and Queen, and everyone in the kingdom lived happily ever after.

Here is a nursery rhyme to go with the story, adapted by Sharifa Oppenheimer:

Little Jenny Wren fell sick upon a time,
In came Robin Redbreast and brought her cake and wine.
"Eat well of my cake, Jenny. Drink well of my wine."
"Thank you, Robin, kindly. You shall be mine."

Jenny she got better and stood upon her feet.
She told Robin plainly she loved him quite a bit.
Robin, being happy, flew up to a tree,
Singing, "Soon we shall be married, hey-diddle-dee!"

RESOURCES

Olive Beaupre Miller, My Book House, Vol. 1 *(Chicago: The Book House for Children 1920).*

Stories for Times in Need of Special Care

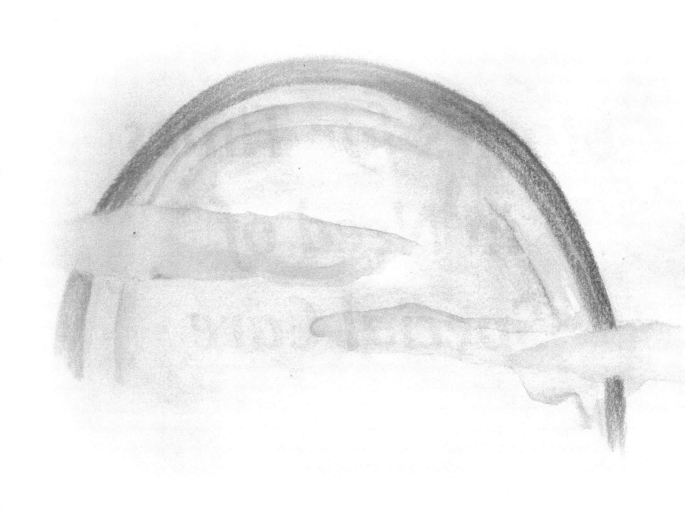

The First Months of Life

SUSAN STARR

Susan has offered workshops where teachers and parents make soft, nine-inch baby knot dolls. She then performs this little story using the dolls they have made. We can easily see this as a wonderful activity in parent-infant and parent-child groups.

ONE DAY, A MOTHER AND A FATHER went out to their favorite place to walk—a lovely meadow. In the meadow, they sent a wish into the blue sky. Their wish was for a child to come to live with them, and the white clouds above them heard and received their wish and sent it all the way into heaven.

But first the clouds brought down a blanket of snow that covered the ground for many, many days. And when the season came for the sun to climb higher in the sky, all the snow melted away, filling creeks and streams everywhere.

The warm sun on the land brought back all the meadow and woodland flowers. And one day, when the mother and father went for a walk in the meadow, they saw a little bundle wrapped in soft colors waiting for them. As they unwrapped their gift from heaven, they saw that their wish had come true, for there sleeping inside was a little baby just for them.

With gentle hands the little baby was rocked and lullabies were sung. It had been a long journey down the rainbow bridge and the little baby needed much sleep in dreamland.

But one day, the baby began to wiggle in their arms, wanting to see more of the new world, so they put her down on her belly and she lifted her wobbly head to look about. Not long afterwards, she was able to push herself up to see even further. Mother Earth was so firm beneath her! When she was turned over and laid on her back, she discovered her feet and hands could all come together. Many sounds of joy were made as she played with her own hands and feet.

One day, while on her back, she saw something beside her that she wanted to touch, so she began to rock and roll, back and forth, and rolled all the way over to grasp and play with the toy.

Another day came when the baby wanted to see and touch more, and she rolled all the way over. She could even push herself up and off her belly to rock forward and backward.

One day she rocked so hard that she pushed herself all the way up and found that she was sitting. How different the world looked now! How free her hands were to pick up and bring everything nearer to herself. From here, the little one could watch and smile at all who loved her as they moved about.

But all babies still want to be picked up and held. And be rocked to sleep and dream the soft dreams of when they lived above. Good night, little baby and family. Good night, meadow.

The Littlest Bear and the Leaf

KATE LAWES

The children Kate encounters love this to cheer on the little bear in this story. They all can relate to her in some way. It also helps the little ones to feel comfortable joining in with the older children. The story also reaches out to parents who may be feeling anxious about letting their young children have space to play.

ONCE UPON A TIME, there was a little brown bear named Norah. She lived deep in a beautiful forest full of Grand Firs and Big Leaf Maples.

Norah was the smallest cub with three brothers, and because of this she spent a lot of time being protected by Mamabear. Norah sat and watched as her mama caught salmon in the stream, and followed along while her mama picked berries from the bushes. Norah never strayed far. She loved learning all the big bear ways.

But as Norah got older, she noticed that all her brother bears were out playing games, and she was still sitting with Mamabear. She could see all the fun her brothers were having, but could not join in because her mama said she was too small. She didn't want her to hurt herself, so she had to stay close and safe.

But one day, when she and Mamabear were resting in the golden sun of an autumn day, Norah heard her brothers playing. She felt she had rested long enough and asked Mamabear if she could go watch the others play. Her mama said she could, just for a little while. "But stay with the other bears and don't stray beyond the creek!"

Norah's brothers were all playing catch-the-falling-leaves. It was so much fun to watch them race about and catch the leaves. And then she spotted a huge yellow leaf floating down. None of the other bears seemed to have spotted it. She thought it would be so nice to catch a leaf! Perhaps she should try.

So Norah slowly got up and started to follow the leaf as it went this way and that way. She had her head up, and followed along very nicely until she tripped and hurt her paw.

But did that stop her? No!

Norah kept her eyes on that leaf and kept going. The wind took it up and down and pushed it all around, but Norah just kept right on following that leaf. She felt her paws squish in some cool mud and brush against some scratchy black berry bushes, but she kept on chasing that leaf. She was so close, and had almost caught it, when the wind changed the direction of the leaf again.

Norah was getting tired. But she thought that surely the leaf would come close to the ground soon and she would be able to catch it. It was such a beautiful leaf! She could show it to Mamabear when she caught it, she thought.

And then all of a sudden she felt herself tumbling!

Norah hadn't realized she had reached the edge of the creek. She tumbled down the bank and, with a splash, landed in the middle of the creek. What a cold, wet, and rough landing, but somehow even this did not stop Norah. She got up quickly, as her only thought was of the leaf.

"Where is the leaf?" Norah looked up, and sure enough it was still floating right above her. She kept her eyes on it as it twisted this way and that. It was floating down! She focused her eyes, she strained her tired muscles, and jumped.

As she stretched out, she felt the leaf touch her paw, and she closed her wet muddy claws around that beautiful yellow leaf. She did it! She caught that leaf!

She slowly opened her paw and looked in awe. It was the most beautiful thing she had ever seen. And then she heard another sound. A cheer went up and she pulled her gaze away from the leaf to see her brothers at the top of the creek bank cheering. And there too, behind them, was Mamabear smiling.

Norah, her brothers, and Mamabear realized that day that though Norah was small, she could run and play in her own way with the other little bears. And though Norah was always the littlest bear in her family, each day that she played catch-the-leaf or jump-over-the-creek or climb-the-tree she got stronger and climbed higher, and learned more and more about what she could do each time she tried.

The Little Boy Who Had Adventures KATHY FRASER

This story, which was inspired by a workshop with Cynthia Lambert and Karen Viani, is one that Kathy often tells at the beginning of the school year to introduce the concept of trying new things, considering before acting, and recognizing one's own readiness for change. It leads right into rest time.

ONCE THERE WAS A LITTLE BOY just about your age, and he decided he was ready to have adventures. So he got into his little bed-boat and set sail across the shining sea.

Hum a little drifting tune.

Soon, he came to an island that was covered in golden sand. He thought to himself, "It might be fun to dig in golden sand."

So he climbed out of his boat, pulled out a shovel he'd brought, and began to make holes and ditches, and to build sand castles and roads. After a while, he grew tired.

> *"Digging in golden sand is lots of fun,*
> *but I am ready for more adventures under the sun."*

He got back into his little boat and sailed across the shining sea.

Hum the same little drifting tune, or a variation.

Soon, he came to an island that was covered in tall green banana trees. He thought to himself, "It might be fun to climb trees and eat bananas."

So he got out of his boat, climbed up the biggest, greenest tree and picked yellow bananas to eat. By and by, he grew tired.

"Climbing banana trees is lots of fun,
digging in golden sand is lots of fun,
but I am ready for more adventures under the sun."

He got back into his little boat and sailed across the shining sea.

Hum the same little drifting tune, or a variation.

Soon, he came to an island that was covered in giant boulders. He thought to himself, "It might be fun to jump on those great big rocks."

So he climbed out of his boat, and onto a boulder. He jumped from one rock to another, hid between them and climbed all over them. After a while, he grew tired.

"Jumping on giant boulders is lots of fun,
climbing banana trees is lots of fun,
digging in golden sand is lots of fun,
but I am ready for more adventures under the sun."

He got back into his little boat and sailed across the shining sea.

Hum the same little drifting tune, or a variation.

Soon, he came to an island with many sparkling ponds and creeks. He thought to himself, "It might be fun to splash in all that sparkling water."

So he got out of his boat and jumped right into the water with all his clothes on, splashing, floating, diving and swimming. By and by, he grew tired.

"Splashing in sparkling water is lots of fun,
jumping on giant boulders is lots of fun,
climbing banana trees is lots of fun
and digging in golden sand is lots of fun,
but (YAWN) now I am tired and when I need rest,
my little bed-boat is what I like best."

He got back into his little bed-boat and sailed across the shining sea, all the way back to his dear mother, who tucked him under his big blue blanket as he drifted off to dream land.

Play the lyre or hum a lullaby.

Nikolai, the Woodcarver

RUTH KER

This story was created as a simple lap-puppet play in order to be able to model gentle handling for the moveable toys which Rudolf Steiner recommended for young children. Having a collection of Russian toys, Ruth discovered that many children treated them roughly at first. However, after hearing the story of Nikolai, and seeing her model tender gestures toward the matrouschka dolls, the children were able to handle the toys more gently themselves.

ONCE THERE WAS A WOODCARVER named Nikolai, who was a good friend of Babouschka's. He also loved to make good toys just like Babouschka does. People said he made the best matrouschka dolls in town.

Everyone in town admired and trusted Nikolai. They said he was so strong and careful because as a young boy he had spent so much time outside. Every day he would ride his bicycle to the tundra and play there among the hills and ponds, tall grasses and flowers. When he arrived home at night, his Mom and Dad would take him onto their laps and hug him as he told the stories of the adventures of his day.

Now Nikolai was older, and he still liked to play—and work! The people in town would visit his shop just to see the beautiful toys and the dolls he made. Sometimes a visitor would be lucky enough to see Nikolai finish making the last little matrouschka doll and then he would kiss life into all of them together.

He would say:

Here, show the smallest Baboushka doll.

"Dear little Valerianna, you are very precious. You are made from the heart of the tree."

Kiss the doll and set it down. Pick up the second smallest doll.

"Dear Yelena, please look after Valerianna."

Kiss Yelena and sit her down beside Valerianna. Pick up the third doll.

"Dear Irena, please look after Yelena."

Kiss Irena—pronounced "ih-ree-nah"—and sit her down beside the rest in line. Repeat words and gesture with the fourth and fifth dolls, Natashya and Nadia—pronounced "naw-dee-ah."

Then Nikolai, when he was finished with his dolls, would remind them again and again about their important tasks.

Begin to nest the dolls one inside the other while continuing to tell the story.

"Remember, Yelena, you look after Valerianna, and Irena, you look after Yelena, and Natashya, you look after Irena and Nadia . . . You are the mother of them all. You must look after all of them."

Then he would wrap up his dolls in a warm blanket. Nikolai would carefully carry them down to the harbour and they would sail across the ocean in a big ship. "Carry my love across the sea," he would say to the captains of the big ships.

Now there was one time that one of Nikolai's toys arrived on the shore of another land. A toy store owner came to the harbor collect some toys that day, and she also chose to take Nadia, Natashya, Irena, Yelena and Valerianna back to her store.

The storekeeper picked the toys up with her rough hands. "Come on, come on," she said. "Get on with it! Give me those bothersome dolls so I can get on with my work!"

The dolls could feel her twitching fingers as she stuffed them into her hand bag. Not only that, the storekeeper had just finished her lunch and her hands were still sticky and dirty from the food she had eaten.

That's the first thing the toys noticed when they were roughly unpacked and placed on the toy shelf at the store. Nadia had bread crumbs on her and the rest of the dolls were covered in places with sticky honey. Not only that! When the storekeeper placed the toys on the shelf, she was very rough with them and she knocked over Valerianna and didn't pick her up. "Oh, where are Nikolai's gentle hands?" said the dolls.

Nevertheless Nadia, Natashya, Irena, Yelen,a and Valeriana were very happy to have a place on the toy store shelf. Many people came to see them.

One day, a little girl came into the toy store with her Mom. She grabbed the toys one by one and set them down impatiently. Before she was finished, poor Yelena was lying sideways, too.

"I want a toy right now!" said the little girl.

"Not today, dear," said her mother, but the girl stomped her feet and began to cry and she took a toy anyway. Her mother paid for the toy and took her out of the store quickly. The dolls were happy that the little girl didn't choose them.

A little while later, Mary came into the toy store. Mary saw Valerianna and Yelena lying sideways. She helped them right away by gently picking them up and arranging them carefully on the shelf. The dolls could feel her kind hands as she ran her fingers over them.

"Oh mother," said Mary, "look at these beautiful dolls. May I have them please?"

"Mary, we do not have enough money right now. Perhaps you can save some money for this yourself," said mother. "I wish I could buy them for you, Mary."

The dolls were very sad to see Mary and her mother leave the store, but before Mary left, she went to the dolls and said, "I'll come back for you, I promise."

Every day after that, the dolls waited for Mary to return. It took a long time. But one day, Mary came back to the store and gave the store keeper some money for the dolls.

Then she came over to the shelf to gather them, saying,

"Now Valerianna, you are made from the heart of the tree and you are special."

Kiss Valerianna.

"Yelena, your task is to look after Valerianna."

Kiss Yelena.

"Irena, your task is to look after Yelena."

Kiss Irena.

"Natashya, your task is to look after Irena."

Kiss Natashya.

"Nadia, your task is to look after Natashya and everyone. You are the mother of them all."

Kiss Nadia.

And Mary and her mother took the toys home with them. Mary cared for them with her kind and gentle hands for ever after that.

Mama's Bed

MARY NATALE

Mary finds this story very helpful when trying to get the children to really rest at naptime.

Mama's bed was enormous! It towered so high, Juniper needed her step ladder to climb up. She could jump much higher on Mama's bed because it was firm. The bed sat on round, stubby legs which looked like tree stumps. Juniper's bed, on the other hand, sat on tall spindle legs. Juniper liked how there was very little space beneath Mama's bed. Trolls couldn't hide there the way they could hide under hers.

A thick, warm, soft quilt, which Grandma had lovingly sewn by hand, adorned the bed. It was dotted with colourful flowers. Sometimes Juniper imagined she was in a beautiful meadow as she lay sprawled upon it. Then she'd jump off and gleefully skip around the room singing, "Oh how I love this bed, oh how I love this bed, oh how I love this bed; it's so comfy!"

Late one stormy night when the wind howled and the rain roared, Juniper ran into Mama's room crying, "Mama, Mama, Mama! There's a troll under my bed!"

Mama wrapped Juniper in her arms and told her there was no troll under her bed or in their safe, cozy home. Slowly she walked Juniper back to her room and together they looked under the bed, but that did not comfort Juniper, and she cried even louder than before. Mama then carried Juniper back to her bed and covered her with the thick, warm, soft quilt. Nestled between Mama and Papa, Juniper felt just right, and in no time, she fell asleep.

Night after night, Juniper ran from her bedroom to Mama and Papa. Then one evening Papa told Juniper a story about a troll who was sad because he did not have any friends. He wanted so much to play with the children of the village but whenever they saw him they would run away crying. At the end of the story Juniper announced that she would like to be the troll's friend. Papa brought her some paper and crayons. He suggested she draw a picture for the troll. Juniper happily coloured a rainbow filling the whole page. She told Papa to write, "Troll, I will be your friend, from Juniper." The next day the rainbow picture, which was left on the front porch rocking chair, was gone and in its place was a banana muffin with a note from the troll. It said, "Thank you for being my friend, Juniper. I hope you like the banana muffin." Juniper was delighted she now had a troll friend. "Mama, Papa," Juniper shouted, "my troll friend makes yummy banana muffins!"

For a while Juniper slept in her bedroom without waking up during the night. Then one evening, frightened by a nightmare, Juniper ran into Mama's room. Mama lifted Juniper into her arms, tucked her into the bed and covered her with the thick, warm, soft quilt. Nestled between Mama and Papa Juniper felt just right, and in no time, she fell asleep.

The next morning Mama woke up with a wonderful idea that she shared with Papa and Grandma. For a few days after dinner Papa took Juniper for a leisurely walk through the woods while Mama and Grandma lovingly sewed a beautiful quilt for Juniper's bed. It was thick, warm, soft and dotted with colourful flowers. When the quilt was finished Mama made Juniper's bed and lay the beautiful quilt on top. Under the bed she tucked a surprise.

After Juniper brushed her teeth Mama walked her to her bedroom. "Mama, Mama, Mama!" shouted Juniper, "I have a quilt on my bed! It's just like yours. Look at all the beautiful flowers!"

Juniper joyfully jumped on her bed and quickly changed into her pyjamas. Mama tucked Juniper into her bed. First she pulled up the peach cotton sheet to her chin. Then she pulled up the woollen blanket and finally the flowered quilt. Juniper was warm all over.

While the candle flickered and filled the room with a soft glow, Mama sat on Juniper's bed and told her a story of the flower fairies. They help children throughout the day and at night; they keep them safe while they sleep. At the end of the story, Mama quietly gave Juniper the surprise. It was a flower fairy doll that she and Grandma lovingly sewed together. She was light with soft petal wings, a bright flowered dress, and long, wavy hair. She fit snugly in Juniper's arms. "Mama, she's beautiful!" whispered Juniper. Mama smiled, gently rubbed her back and quietly sang, "Fairy light, fairy bright, I will hold you tight. Fairy light, fairy bright, I am safe all the night." Mama sang this sweet lullaby over and over. Soon Juniper, feeling warm and just right, fell asleep and slept soundly throughout the night.

Twinkle

NANCY FORER

Another story for transitioning into sleep. For a lap puppet show you will need a simple hand-held "fellow" dressed in pajama-like clothes and a night cap. He can be tucked into a silk or the folds of a child's blanket.

Way up high in the sky at night
A fluffy cloud covers Twinkle tight.

He wakes to do his job so fine,
Polishing stars to make them shine.

He stretches and yawns, then off he goes,
From star to star on his swift toes.

He polishes stars till they shine bright
He rubs and works all through the night.

And when bright sun lights up the skies,
Back to a cloud Twinkle flies.

He covers up, then goes to sleep.
Little Twinkle makes not a peep.

"Sshhhh, little Twinkle," we whisper, "Good night!
"Sshhhh, little Twinkle, You sleep tight."

Variation: at naptime, you may prefer to use the following:

"Sshhhh, Little Twinkle, you worked through the night.
Sshhhh, Little Twinkle, now you sleep tight."

Sing a closing song, such as "Twinkle, Twinkle, Little Star"

A Bridge of Hope

KAYTI HENRY

This was written for a child whose parents were going through a particularly difficult divorce.

ONCE UPON A TIME, in a far off land, there was a kingdom of shadows. All who lived within this kingdom could never truly be happy, not even the king and queen, for the sun never shone there. The dark clouds in the sky filled the people's hearts with sorrow, and they walked through each day with a heaviness that no one knew how to lift.

One day, a terrible storm broke out. Thunder rumbled and roared so loudly that the people in the kingdom had to hide inside their homes. Jagged bolts of lightning cut through the dark clouds in the sky, bringing blinding flashes of light. Then the rain began to fall, starting as a light drizzle, and getting harder and stronger until it poured down from the sky in great torrents. For many days the raging storm continued, until the kingdom began to flood. A river formed, rushing and crashing its way through the middle of the kingdom. It even tore through the castle, leaving the king on one side and the queen on the other.

Time passed, and the storm subsided. The thunder and lightning ceased, and a gentle drizzle was all that remained. All the people of the kingdom were finally able to venture forth from their homes. As they looked about, they saw all the damage the storm had brought. Trees were uprooted, and roads and pathways through the kingdom had been completely washed away. The people also noticed that a river had formed that split the kingdom in two. When the people realized this, they did not know what to do. The river was too wide and deep to swim across. How would they ever see their friends who lived on the other side of the river?

Then, the eldest and wisest of the kingdom said, "Let us ask the king, surely he will know what to do!"

And on the other side of the river, a young child said, "Let us go and ask the queen, for surely she will know what to do."

So the people on both sides of the river walked through the drizzling rain to the castle.

When the people from one side of the river arrived, the king welcomed them. He listened patiently to their worries, while on the other side of the river, the queen was listening to the worries of the people there. The king and queen each said, "If only there was a bridge over the river, then we could cross it . . ."

Just then, a light shone forth through the gray sky. This was the first light the kingdom had ever seen. The people were amazed. As they gazed at the light, they felt their sorrows and worries melting away. A new warmth and joy seemed to fill their hearts. As the light in the sky grew, something most wonderful appeared over the river. It was a bridge of many colors, and it stretched all the way from one side of the river to the other.

As they gazed at the rainbow bridge in amazement, everyone began to cheer. They were overjoyed, for though the river still stood between them, they now had a way to cross over it.

A Place for a Baby to Sleep

KELLY MARIE BARHAM

Through fairy images and images from nature, this story of two tomtens' quest tells a refugee's tale.

One winter day, two little tomtens with nowhere to live were wandering around in the forest, looking for a place to rest. They were wishing for the Christmas fairies to bring them a baby to keep, but they did not have a place where a baby could sleep.

They saw Squirrel Nutkin in a fine big tree house, and they knocked politely at the door.

"Good afternoon, Squirrel Nutkin, friend, we are so cold, may we please come in? We are hoping for a baby to keep, but we first need a place where a baby can sleep."

Squirrel Nutkin shook his head and chattered, "Oh no! Can't you see? My house is full of acorns for me! There is not room for anything more, so go away friend, knock on some other door!"

The two little tomtens were surprised. But they could see that there were so many acorns in the house, no one could even get through the door.

So on they trudged, with their feet getting sore.

They looked up into the hills and saw Mother Bear's cave house. The snow was sparkling in the afternoon sun, and they thought, a cave could be a cozy place to rest. Surely Mother Bear would offer them space in her warm nest.

They called up in their sweetest voices, and the bells on their hats jingled merrily.

"Mother Bear! Mother Bear! Are you at home? We are two tomtens, cold and alone! We are hoping for a baby to keep, but we first need a place where a baby can sleep."

Mother Bear came out rumbling and grumbling, and she began to shout, "My cave is full of cubs this year, can't you see? So go away now, and don't bother me!"

Sad little tomtens, they walked on. And as the sun began to hide its face, they hoped to find just one more place. Across a bridge, they saw a light, and hoped for a home before it grew night.

As they got closer, they thought perhaps it was the home of Brother Skunk. They could see his beautiful bushy black and white tail through the window. They saw his warm fireplace, and his merrily decorated walls.

"Surely, he is expecting special guests this evening," said Mr. Tomten. "Perhaps we should not bother him."

But Mrs. Tomten was so tired, she wanted to knock once more.

Brother Skunk came hurrying out. "Dear tomtens! Why are you wandering around in the dark, so cold and alone? Come right in, my home is your home! I have been hoping for visitors, come and see, the fireplace is warm, there is soup, and some bread. And a wee little place to lay your sweet head."

The tomtens said, "Thank you! What a kind friend, indeed."

And when they had eaten, and snuggled up tight, the Christmas fairies came flying through the sparkling night. A gift they did bring, the best gift of all . . .

A baby to keep.

For now they had a place where a baby could sleep.

Chippy and His Family

CAROL GRIEDER-BRANDENBERGER

This story was written to help families with the topic of adoption.

ONCE UPON A TIME, out at the edge of the forest where many oak and birch trees grew, where the sun reached into every corner of the forest and the leaves of the trees offered protection from rain and snow, there was a chipmunk village. In this village there lived many chipmunk families and one of them included a mother and a father and a little chipmunk child named Chippy.

Every morning when the sun rose, little Chippy the chipmunk poked his nose out of the hole and sniffed the fresh air. It was a new day! He quickly settled down at the table with his family to eat a breakfast of nuts and seeds. Then he hugged his mother and father goodbye and scampered off to school to work and play with all of his chipmunk friends from the village.

He had many friends, and they had much in common: The stripes on their backs, their soft brown eyes, their bushy tails and their love for nuts and acorns. And even though the chipmunks had so much in common, they were also quite different. Some had darker and other lighter stripes, some had fluffy long fur and others had shorter and straight fur. Some of the little chipmunks liked to scamper joyfully while others enjoyed walking more deliberately. Some had many little chipmunk brothers and sisters and others had many little chipmunk friends.

Some lived with their grandparents while others lived with one mother or with one father, or with two mothers or two fathers. And others lived with both a mother and a father. Some arrived into their families by being born into them and others by being adopted into them. And all had one thing in common: In each of the families there was love for each other.

One day, Chippy asked his mother: "Tell me again about the day I was born." Chippy's mother loved to tell him about that special day, and so she sat down once again to share with him the story of his birth:

"Once upon a time, there was a mother and a father, and a happy little chipmunk. They lived together with much joy and love. In fact, there could have not been more love in this family, because the little chipmunk came into the family through the help of a birth mother and birth father chipmunk who at that time in their lives could not raise a chipmunk baby. Sometimes it takes many chipmunks to help a little baby chipmunk come over the rainbow bridge onto this earth, where the sun shines and the wind blows and the rain can fall hard, and where little Chippy had wished to be born into. These two kind and caring chipmunks were part of the rainbow bridge which helped little Chippy find his family, who had been waiting for him.

"So the little chipmunk baby crossed over the rainbow bridge and was placed into the arms of his mother and father who had been hoping and waiting for him for a long time, and who adopted him.

"After his birth, which was a great celebration, his chipmunk mother and father took little baby chipmunk home and cared for him, and their home was filled with much love, goodness and joy."

When little Chippy was born he did not know about this very special birth story. Once he grew older he learned the meaning of the word adoption. It helped him feel even more connected to his family, and loved and treasured.

Little Chippy asked: "What does adoption mean?" "Adoption means that I love you. Adoption means we are a 'forever' family," said his mother, and gave him a big chipmunk hug.

Little Chippy loved to hear the story of his birth. He loved his family. He was thankful that his birth parents had helped create the rainbow bridge that brought him to his family. He gave his mother a hug and scampered off to play with his friends outside, until the dinner bells rang and the sun set over the chipmunk village.

Flame

SACHA ETZEL

For all those displaced by fires.

NOT SO FAR AWAY AND NOT SO LONG AGO, there was a dry desert land where Brother Wind blew gently upon the land and upon all Mother Earth's creatures. This desert land had many tall, fragrant eucalyptus trees and small little bushes covering it. Many creatures called this desert home.

The birds lived high in the trees and watched over the land and its creatures. They flew from tree to tree. Coyote could often be seen looking for small creatures to eat. Wild bushy-tailed bunnies hopped on two feet, eating anything green they could find. And deer could sometimes be seen eating leaves from the bushes and trees. Even though there was hardly any water, this was good land and the animals were happy living here.

One day, a spark of flame leaped out of Father Sun and landed on a bush. The bush began to burn.

Brother Wind blew and blew and blew and Flame grew bigger and taller and hotter. Flame jumped to a nearby bush, and then to another, and each time Flame jumped, it grew bigger and hotter. It wasn't long before Flame was as tall as the eucalyptus trees!

Oh, my! The animals did not know what to do; they did not understand that Flame wanted to give new life to that land. They called on Sister Rain to shed her tears. But Sister Rain could not come. They asked Brother Wind to stop blowing on Flame, but Brother Wind understood the ways of that land, and kept on blowing.

"What shall we do?" asked the animals.

Flame grew so big and so very hot that the animals grew very afraid. They could no longer live in their burrows or dens or branches; Flame was burning them all. There was only one thing the animals could do, and that was to leave their homes and find shelter somewhere else. And so the bunnies, coyotes, deer, and birds all ran as fast as they could, for they could feel Flame's heat coming ever closer.

Full of fear, they ran and they ran. They could not stop, though they were so very tired, until they had left Flame far behind. At last they came to the beach where Mother Earth was rolling her waves against the shore. There they rested, knowing that wise Mother Earth held everything in her bosom and that Father Sun spread his warm light upon the land. Here they were safe at last.

After they had rested they realized that they no longer had homes to live in.

"My nest has surely fallen from the branch and been burned," said the bird.

"My hole is certainly full of ash and smoke," said the bunny.

"My den is destroyed," said the coyote.

And the deer, who spoke very rarely, knew that her soft, grassy bed had been turned to cinders.

All the animals were sad and bewildered because they had lost their homes. Flame was destroying everything!

Wise Mother Earth embraced them and Father Sun encircled them with his warm light. The animals huddled together and listened to Mother Earth rolling her waves against the shore. They took deep breaths and were very quiet and still together.

Back in the desert land, Flame saw that almost everything was gone—the trees, the bushes, all the animals' homes, and even the earth were black. Flame knew that for there to be new life, all the old had to be taken away. Flame looked all around and saw that its work was done. A new land had been created. Flame leaped into Mother Earth's big bountiful ocean as she rolled her waves over Flame, holding Flame close to her heart.

Sister Rain sent rain to cool the burnt earth at last. Soon the animals could return to this new land. Already grasses were growing, stronger and greener than before. The shrubs grew back, bushier and fuller than they had ever been, and the trees sent out new branches and new saplings. The land had been made new!

Bunny burrowed down into the cool earth and coyote dug a new den. The birds once again built nests in the branches of the trees and bushes, and deer once again lay in her grassy bed. Brother Wind gently blew Mother Earth's soft ocean breeze upon all the creatures who were happily home again under Father Sun's warm sky.

A Reverse Rainbow Bridge Story JENNY TAYLOR

This story was written for a six-year-old child who had recently experienced traumatic events, including the suicide of a parent. It is based on the story typically used in the Waldorf kindergarten classroom for birthday celebrations.

THERE WAS ONCE A LITTLE ONE who crossed the rainbow bridge and became a child of the Earth. When he was a baby, he remembered his home in the clouds where the sun always shone, and the rains never fell, and the breezes were gentle and warm. But as he grew, his head became too full of the colors, and people, and music of the earth to have room for such things.

The Little One became a boy. He loved his mother and father and sisters and brothers, and they loved him. He made friends, he played, he worked, and he learned. Most of his days were sunny and happy. When storms came, they never lasted long. He remembered his Big Angel, and felt the Angel close by.

The Little One grew into a young man. He forgot about his Big Angel, but still, the angel was always there. He had adventures—sometimes fun and sometimes difficult. He was brave, and he worked hard; he learned to listen and to speak. He fell in love, and was joined on the earth by Little Ones of his own, whom he loved with all his heart. He had many bright days, when it was easy to be good and kind and strong. But some days were dark: the rains fell, and the breezes felt hard and cold. On those days it was harder to remember how to be a Golden Knight. But then his Big Angel would whisper words of courage and strength in his ear and help blow the clouds away.

One dark, cold, rainy day the Little One, who was now a grown man, was sitting in his favorite place on the Earth, looking out over the water. On this day, his Big Angel whispered in his ear, "It is time to come home." And then the man saw his Big Angel standing beside him, and he saw the Rainbow Bridge stretching out over the water and up into the heavens.

The Little One who had become a man of the Earth remembered his home in the clouds with the warm sun and the gentle breezes and felt a longing in his heart to return. But he also wanted to stay with his family on the earth. His Big Angel smiled at him and said, "Don't worry, even when they cannot see you, you will always be there to guard them and to guide them. Then his Big Angel gave him a hug and took him by the hand, and together they crossed the Rainbow Bridge. When they arrived in the clouds, the Big Angel gave the Man a beautiful pair of feathery wings. "You are a Big Angel now, too." And he was.

RESOURCES

Barbara Patterson, Pamela Bradley, and Jean Riordan, Beyond the Rainbow Bridge *(Amesbury, Massachusetts: Michaelmas Press 2000).*

Returning to the Heavenly Gardens LAUREN HICKMAN

Lauren developed this adaptation of the traditional Rainbow Bridge story to address the needs of parents and others in talking to children about the death of a loved one—not for the classroom, but rather to offer at memorial services and other remembrance gatherings. She has found that this simple story, appropriate for young children, gives great comfort and a sense of meaning to people of all ages sharing in loss and love.

The storyteller adds gender-related pronouns, the Heavenly Child's name, and other details where indicated, or as desired.

ONCE UPON A TIME IN THE HEAVENLY GARDENS, there lived a wise Heavenly Child who loved to play and sing with the other heavenly children. One day the Child was walking along the heavenly path when the clouds billowed up and separated, and she looked down upon the Earth. There were gardens and trees, rivers and oceans below. It looked so beautiful that she wanted to go there.

The Child went to the angels and said, "Please, may I go to that beautiful world?"

The angels put their arms around the Child and said, "Wait, it is not time yet."

So the wise Heavenly Child played with the other heavenly children in the heavenly gardens.

Now it happened that one day that the Child was walking along the heavenly path when she noticed a chink in the heavenly wall. She went up and looked through the chink. There was a little house with tall trees and rosebushes. In the house were a mother and father.

"Ah," they said, "If only we could have a child! Maybe the Good God would grant us one."

There they were, doing everything they could to prepare for a baby, making sure there was a home with a baby bed, and that all the baby clothes were soft and clean. There were grandparents, too, waiting for a baby. When the Child saw there was so much love and joy in their waiting home, she wanted to go there too.

The Child ran back to the angels and said, "I have found my parents! Please may I go there now?"

The angels put their arms around the Child and said, "You may go, but the journey will be one which takes great courage and strength."

The Child stood up straight and tall, looked the angels in the eyes with courage and said, "I will take this journey. I am ready to go now."

The angels said, "You may go. The first part of your journey is to travel to the houses of the sun, the moon, and the stars. At each house, you will have a special task. This is all in preparation for your journey."

The Child prepared for the journey, hugged the angels, and set forth.

The Child traveled to the house of the stars where she learned how to polish them with the softest cloth until they twinkled and sparkled so beautifully in the night time sky. For the Child's hard work, she received the gift of starlight in her eyes.

Next the Child traveled to the house of Mother Moon. Carefully, she polished the moon's round, silver face with the softest cloth until it shone with all its full moon beauty. Mother Moon bestowed on the Child the gift of wisdom.

Finally, the Child traveled to the house of Father Sun. She polished and polished the face of Father Sun with the softest cloth until it shown with the brilliance of the midday sun. For this hard work, the Child received the greatest gift of all, the gift of love which she was to bring to Earth.

Now the Heavenly Child traveled through a meadow full of flowers. She picked a big basket full of flowers which turned out to be quite heavy. She stood up with full courage, lifted the heavy basket, and headed towards a tall mountain. She climbed to the top of the mountain, and in the distance saw a glittering silver lake. The Child knew that was where she needed to go, and traveled all day, carrying the heavy basket until she reached the shores of the lake. There the Child sat down to rest for a while.

The sun was setting, the mama birds were singing their nighttime songs to their babies, and the mama frogs sang their lullabies too. Just then, what do you think the Child saw? A beautiful white swan swam up, and the Child jumped on her back, holding fast to her graceful white neck. Together they swam out into the middle of the lake, where there was a beautiful, pinky-peachy colored water lily.

The Heavenly Child jumped into the center of the water lily. There she met a big angel who rocked her all night long.

In the morning, when the sun rose, the water lily opened its petals and the Child's own big angel said, "Give me your heavenly garments. You will not need them where you are going. Give them to me and I shall keep them until you return."

Carefully, the Heavenly Child took off the heavenly garments, folded them and gave them to the big angel who tucked them under his wing, and together they walked to the top of the rainbow bridge.

The angel gave just the tiniest push, and down, down the Heavenly Child slid.

But she was no longer a Heavenly Child, she was a beautiful baby. Down, down she slid, into her mother's arms. Her father was there too, and together they said, "What would be the very best name for our baby?"

A template for the Child's story follows. This will be familiar to teachers who celebrate birthday stories in the Waldorf kindergarten and nursery.

_____ was her name.

_____ was such a beautiful baby, with ten pink fingers and toes. Mama and Papa loved her so much.

Add further life details here to give a picture of the Child's life, such as things the Child liked to do, and things that others like to do with him or her. For instance, "The Child grew up to be a parent to [names of children] and loved to play catch with her children. Her work was..." and so on.

Now it came to pass that one day, the angels called the Child's name, and it was time to return to the heavenly gardens. The Child made sure that everyone knew she loved them, and thanked each one who came across her path. Once the Child was sure that her gift of love would be shared on earth, she kissed her loved ones and went back up the rainbow bridge.

The Child's big angel was waiting for her with the heavenly garments she had left behind. The Child's loved ones missed her, but knew that she would always be with them, and the Child knew they would always remember her.

A Story for Finny and Theo

PATRICIA CARLIN

Patricia wrote this story for her students upon the death of one of their classmates. The child's sibling had also been lost.

ONCE THERE WAS A BEAUTIFUL WILLOW TREE that lived in the garden. All the schoolchildren loved to visit the willow tree, and even called her "Mrs. Willow." The willow tree liked that name!

Mrs. Willow was very friendly and generous: the children loved making willow crowns with the feathery branches Mrs. Willow let fall to the ground. When the birds asked if they could make nests in her branches, Mrs. Willow said, "Yes, of course, my pleasure!" When the squirrels asked if they could make nests in her branches, Mrs. Willow said, "Yes, of course, my pleasure!" When the butterflies asked if they could play in her branches, Mrs. Willow said, "Yes, of course, with pleasure!"

When the butterflies walked with their tiny, delicate feet on Mrs. Willow's branches, she said it tickled! But most of all, Mrs. Willow loved watching the butterfly friends play with one another, for each one was good and kind. Sometimes, in their games, the butterflies made tiny houses with twigs and berries on Mrs. Willow's branches. Sometimes, one or two of the butterflies would be "baby butterflies," and the others would be the mommy, daddy, sister, and brother butterflies. Two of the butterflies who had the speediest wings would race around Mrs. Willow's long branches, flying so fast and laughing and laughing. All of the butterfly friends were very happy, and Mrs. Willow was happy too.

One day, a new little butterfly friend arrived at the tree. He was very gentle and watched all of the other butterflies playing. Mrs. Willow was watching, too, and said, "Come, gentle butterfly, and play with all the butterfly friends." The butterfly friends said, "Yes, please play with us, gentle butterfly." And so he did. And he was happy.

Shortly after, a big, loud storm threw many raindrops to the earth. Mrs. Willow called all the butterfly friends to huddle under her leafy umbrellas to stay dry. They stayed close to each other and peered out from under the leaves to watch the storm. In a while, the big storm was over and the bright sun appeared once again in the sky. But some of the raindrops still hovered in the sky, and when the bright sunlight shone through them, a marvelous rainbow appeared.

The butterflies, who love color, were enchanted. As they watched, a second rainbow appeared, and the whole sky was bursting with colors. The butterflies were even more enchanted. One of them said, "Let's fly to the rainbows and dive into the colors!"

One by one, the butterflies launched themselves upward, saying, "Good-bye, Mrs. Willow! We'll be back soon!"

But it is not so easy to fly to a rainbow, for it is very far away in the sky. One by one, the delicate wings of each butterfly grew tired, and most of the butterflies turned around and flew wearily back to Mrs. Willow.

But not the gentle butterfly. He flew all the way to the rainbow, and it was so beautiful and its colors were so grand that he decided to stay there. When he opened his wings, they became glorious rainbow wings, and he became the rainbow butterfly.

All the Willow butterfly friends missed their friend, the gentle butterfly, and wished that he would come again and play with them. And whenever they saw a rainbow, they remembered their gentle friend. And if they looked very carefully, they really could see their friend inside the rainbow, shining light and goodness onto the world.

Stories
for Anytime

The Little Duckling

NANCY FORER

This is for a simple puppet story for infants and toddlers. Props that may be used are silk cloths, knitted ducks, felted fish, and a felted frog.

Storyteller sings:

> Here comes little duckling, walking down the path.
> "Quack-quack," says he.
> Plip-plop go his feet.
> He waddles to the water,
> Then jumps in with a bound.
> Splash-splash! He swims all around.
> Swim, little duckling, in the water blue,
> Swim by the fish, swimming there, too.
> "Ribbet-ribbet." Swim by the frog, sitting on his log.
>
> "Quack-quack-quack," Mama Duck is calling you.
> Swim, little duckling, in the water blue.
> Find Mama Duck. She's looking for you.

Storyteller and children sing together:

> Little Duck and Mama Duck swim in the water blue.
> Swim, little duck, in the water blue,
> Swim with Mama Duck swimming there, too.

Alternative song:

Diddle diddle duddle
Duckie's in the puddle
The little one dips and dives
He splishes, he splashes
He dunks and he dashes
Then follows his Mama behind
Then follows his Mama behind.

Little Cloud

LINDA GRANT

This is a lovely tale to act out, with a piece of carded wool that can easily be shaped to portray the different animals and the cloud.

Once upon a time there was a little cloud. He was a fluffy white cloud, and he loved to float in the blue sky high above the land.

One day, the little cloud looked down and saw the sheep and the lambs in the green fields below. They grazed in the green grass and were happy.

The little cloud said to himself:

"I wish I could be a little lamb grazing in the green fields. How happy I would be!"

The wind blew the little cloud . . .

. . . and hoola, hoola, hoola! The little cloud found himself to be a little lamb! In the green fields he grazed on the grass. The little lamb wandered through the fields, finding the tastiest grasses to eat, and he was very happy.

One day, the little lamb came to a river. He looked into the river and saw the fish swimming freely in the cool water. The little lamb said to himself:

"I wish I could be a fish swimming freely in the cool water. How happy I would be!"

The little lamb leaned forward to drink the water . . .

. . . and hoola, hoola, hoola! He found himself to be a little fish! He swam freely in the cool water of the river. The little fish swam and swam with all the other fish, and he was very happy.

One day as the little fish was swimming, he looked up and saw the clouds floating by in the blue sky overhead. The little fish said to himself:

"I wish I could be a little cloud floating high in the blue sky overhead. How happy I would be!"

The little fish jumped up out of the water to catch a fly, and as he did. . .

. . . hoola, hoola, hoola! He found he was once again a little white cloud. The little white cloud floated high in the blue sky overhead and he was very happy. And he thought to himself:

"I'm happiest as a little white cloud floating high in the blue sky!"

And if I'm not mistaken, he is there to this very day. So if you look up into the blue sky, you will see him—the little, fluffy white cloud floating by.

The Snail and the Butterfly

LOUISE deFOREST, ADAPTED FROM A STORY BY SILVIA JENSEN

A little girl walked in her garden
And the wind whistled around her and told her this story:

Once upon a time there was a dear snail.
She was going for a walk on a golden trail.
Looking here, looking there, and who did she spy?
Lady Flifer, the lovely butterfly!

Said Lady Flifer, "Come fly with me.
Oh the sights you and I will see!
Hop up on my wings and you and I will fly!"
And so she did and they flew up high.

They flew up, they flew down.
Suddenly said the snail:
"What do I see down there?
I see a white hopping hare."

With fingers, show the hare hopping. Repeat: "Hophop, hophop . . ."

They flew up, they flew down
Suddenly said the snail:
"What do I spy behind the log?
I spy a noisy dog!"

The dog barks. Repeat: " woof, woof, woof . . ."

They flew up, they flew down.
Suddenly said the snail:
"What do I spot in that cozy house?
I see a little mouse!"

Twitch noses, mimic sniffing here and there.

They flew up, they flew down
Suddenly said the snail:
"What do I spot in the kitchen?
I see a hungry kitten!"

The cat meows. Repeat: "meow, meow, meow . . ."

They flew up, they flew down.
Suddenly said the snail:
"What do I spot on that big rock?
I see a singing cock!"

The cock crows. Repeat: "cock-a-doodle-doo, cock-a-doodle-doo, cock-a-doodle-doo . . ."

And like this they flew, up and down
Until they finally reached the ground.
"Thank you, dear Flifer, what a wonderful sail!"
And snail went back to her golden trail.

And the girl went back to her home, running fast,
To tell her family all that had passed.

Little Black Cat

REBECCA DAVIS

Once there was a little cat
With eyes of gold and fur all black.
He took a walk outside one day
Looking for a friend to play.

Cat came upon a garden bed
With flowers blooming, pink and red,
And there above them fluttered by
A lovely shining butterfly.

The cat said, "Meow, I want to play!"
The butterfly just flew away.

The little cat then turned around.
He heard a rumbly, bumbly sound.
He saw a fuzzy honey bee
Visiting flowers busily.

The cat said, "Meow, I want to play!"
The honey bee just buzzed away.

Cat wandered on and then did see
A squirrel scamper up a tree.
The squirrel carried acorns sweet
For her hungry babes to eat.

The cat said, "Meow, I want to play!"
But the squirrel just ran away.

At last Cat came to a small gate
Where he could rest, as it was late.
He curled into a tiny ball
Then fell asleep . . . but that's not all . . .

A little girl came down the path,
She'd had her supper and her bath.
She came outside to look around.
She thought she'd heard a meowing sound.

She spied the kitty fast asleep,
Curled up tight right by her feet.
She gently stroked his soft, warm fur.
By and by he began to purr.

The little girl said, "I want to play!"
The black cat said, "With you I'll stay."

The Legend of the Dipper

CAROLYN S. BAILEY

THERE ONCE WAS A LITTLE GIRL who had a dear mother, and they lived quite alone in a little house in the woods. They were always very happy, but one day the mother grew so ill that it seemed as if she could never be strong and well again.

"I must have a drink of clear, cold water," she cried as she lay in her bed, so weak and suffering from thirst.

It was a dark night and there was no one near to ask for water, so the little girl took her tin dipper and started out alone to the spring to bring her mother a drink. She went a long way through the woods, and she ran so that she grew very tired, being such a tiny girl; but she filled the tin dipper at the spring and started home.

Sometimes the water spilled, because it was not easy to carry, and sometimes the little girl stumbled over the stones in the dark path. All at once she felt a warm touch upon her hand and she stopped. It was a little dog who had been following her, for he, too, was nearly dying of thirst, and he had touched her hand with his hot tongue.

The little girl looked at her dipper. There was only a very little water in it, but she poured a few drops into her hand, and let the thirst dog lap them up. He seemed as refreshed as if he had been to the river to drink his fill. And a wonderful thing happened to the tin dipper—although the little girl did not see it. It was changed to a silver dipper, with more water than before.

The little girl started on again, hurrying very fast, for she remembered how much her mother needed her. But she had not gone very far when she met a stranger on the path. He was tall and wore shining garments and his eyes looked down with a wonderful smile into the little girl's face. He reached out his hand for the dipper, and he begged for a drink of the clear, cold water.

Now, the little girl thought how her mother had told her that she should be always kind to a stranger, so she held the water up to his lips. And very suddenly, as the stranger drank, the silver dipper was changed to a gold dipper—full to the brim with sparkling water.

The little girl hurried on, but the road was so very long, and she was so tired, that it seemed as if she could never reach home again. She was weak and faint, and she longed to drink just a few drops of water, but no, her mother would need all that was left. Had she not given some to the thirsty dog and to the stranger? So she never took a drink herself, but hastened home and carried it to her dear mother. And then came the greatest wonder of all! As soon as the mother drank she became quite well and strong again, and the golden dipper, as it touched her lips, was changed to a diamond dipper—all shining and blazing with glittering gems!

And the diamond dipper left her fingers to shine up in the sky, over the house and the woods. There it shines every night to tell the little children how once a child was brave and unselfish and kind.

RESOURCES

Carolyn S. Bailey, For the Children's Hour (Springfield, Massachusetts: Milton-Bradley Company 1906).

A Tool Story

NICKY MARTENS

A kind man goes out to greet the day,
but soon sees that a tree has fallen along his way.
He knows he must move the tree right away
so he can get on with his work and his play.

He goes to his shed which is in quite a mess,
to grab his good saw and put its blade to the test.
But when he reaches the tree and tries to begin,
he realizes he has a shovel with a sharp point at the end.

He tries it to see if it will work.
"Hack and whack, hack and whack, hack and whack!"

The shovel cries out when he stops hacking and whacking,
"I have good work that I love to do,
so use me for my work that is good and true!"

The kind man then sees
a shovel is not for cutting trees.
A shovel is for digging holes in the ground,
sometimes square and sometimes round.

Now he carries the shovel back to his shed
and puts it in its proper place
and this creates a little space,
and so he reaches for his saw
and heads back to the tree that did fall.

But when he reaches the tree and tries to begin,
he realizes he has a rake with points at the end.

He tries it to see if it will work.
"Skritch-scratch, skritch-scratch, skritch-scratch!"

Now the rake cries out when he stops skritching and scratching,
"I have good work that I love to do,
so use me for my work that is good and true!"

The man then sees the rake is not for cutting
but for making piles of leaves beneath the trees.
So he carries the rake back to his shed
and puts it in its proper place
and this creates just a little more space.

So once again he reaches for his saw
and heads back to the tree that did fall.
But when he reaches the tree and tries to begin
he realizes he has a hose with water coming out the end.

He tries it to see if it will work.
"Splish-splash, splish-splash, splish-splash!"

And the hose cries out when he stops splishing and splashing,
"I have good work that I love to do,
so use me for my work that is good and true!"

The man then sees
a hose is good for watering, not cutting trees!

From the water that poured all over the tree
the ground is all muddy and the dirt moves so free,
the man then has a wonderful idea.
The shovel would love to dig in this dirt!

So he goes back to his shed to get the shovel,
so that it can do its good work.
But first he puts the hose in its proper place,
and this creates even more space.

Now having put his tools in their proper place,
his shed is all clean with lots of space
and he can easily reach the shovel, hanging in its place.

So he heads for the tree with shovel in hand
and begins moving the mud and dirt from the ground.
"Crinch-crunch, crinch-crunch, crinch-crunch!"
When all the dirt has been moved away
the tree can be easily set aside.

The work is now done and the kind man can say
that soon he will go on his way.
The shovel then says to him
"I have good work that I love to do,
so thank you
for using me for my work that is good and true!"

And the man, now with a smile on his face,
takes the shovel back to his shed
and puts it in its proper place!

The Little Red Hen

A TRADITIONAL ENGLISH FOLKTALE ADAPTED BY CONNIE MANSON

ONCE THERE WAS A LITTLE CAT, a Little Mouse and . . .
a Little Red Hen.

They lived together in a little cottage in the middle of the forest.
The Little Cat had a soft little basket.
The Little Mouse had a deep little hole.
And the Little Red Hen had a high pole on which she could roost.

One morning, the Little Red Hen awoke and said,
"Now who will rise and light a fire in the wood stove?"
"Not I," said the cat from her basket.
"Not I," said the mouse from his hole.
"Then I will do it myself!" said the little red hen.
And she rose and lit a fire in the wood stove.

And when the fire was lit, the Little Red Hen said,
"And who will sweep the room?"
"Not I," said the Little Cat.
"Not I," said the Little Mouse.
"Then I will sweep the room!" said the Little Red Hen.
And so she did.

And when the room was swept, the Little Red Hen said,
"Now who will step out into the garden and gather the oats for breakfast?"
"Not I," said the Little Cat.
"Not I," said the Little Mouse.

"Then I will gather them myself!" said the Little Red Hen.
And she stepped out into the garden to gather the oats.

No sooner had the Little Red Hen left the little cottage
than who should come waltzing down the road but the Fox,
carrying a sack upon his back.
The Fox knocked at the door.
But the Little Cat did not rise from her soft little basket.
The Little Mouse did not peep out of his deep little hole.
The Fox stepped into the room.
"Good morning, Little Cat, good morning, Little Mouse," said the Fox.

"The Fox!" yowled the Little Cat, and crouched deeper in her basket.
"The Fox!" squeaked the Little Mouse, and ducked deeper into his hole.
They thought they could thus safely hide themselves, but it was to no avail.
The Fox took the Little Cat from her soft little basket,
and the Little Mouse from his deep little hole,
and threw them into the sack.

The Little Red Hen had just finished gathering the oats for breakfast.
She heard the commotion and stepped into the room.
"The Fox!" clucked the Little Red Hen.
Before she could make another sound, the Fox took the Little Red Hen
and threw her into the sack.
He threw the sack over his back and ran down the road.

Now the sun was very hot that day,
and soon the sack became too heavy for the Fox to carry.
He threw it upon the ground and lay down under the shade of a tall tree
and fell asleep. No sooner had the Fox gone to sleep
than the Little Red Hen pulled out from under her wing
a tiny pair of scissors, a spool of thread, and a tiny needle.

"Now who will help me cut open the sack?" she whispered.
"I will," whispered the Little Cat.
"And I will," whispered the Little Mouse.
And so together they snipped a hole in the sack and leapt out.

"Now who will help me gather stones?" asked the Little Red Hen.
"I will," said the Little Cat.
"And I will," said the Little Mouse.
And so each one found a stone as large as themselves
and together they pushed the stones into the sack.

"Now who will help me sew up the sack?" whispered the Little Red Hen.
"I will." whispered the Little Cat.
"And I will," whispered the Little Mouse.
And so together they stitched up the sack and ran back home again.

After some time the Fox awoke.
He pulled the sack over his back and ran down the road with it.
"My, how heavy the sack is to me now," he thought.
The sun was shining even hotter than before. Soon the Fox came to a well.
"I'll get me a drink from this well." he said.

But as he leaned over the well, the sack leaned over, too,
and began to slide down into the well.
"Little Cat, Little Mouse, Little Red Hen, you shan't escape from me!"
the Fox cried, and he grabbed onto the sack and held on tight.
But the three stones that lay inside the sack were so heavy
that they pulled the Fox over the edge, and carried him down into the well.
And the Fox was never heard from again.

When the Little Cat and the Little Mouse and the Little Red Hen
reached the cottage, the Little Red Hen said,
"Now who will help me cook the breakfast?"

"I will," said the Little Cat.
"And I will," said the Little Mouse.
And so together they cooked the breakfast.

"And who will help me set the table?" asked the Little Red Hen.
"I will," said the Little Cat.
"And I will," said the Little Mouse.
And together they set the table.
"And who will help me eat up the breakfast?" asked the Little Red Hen.

"I will!" said the Little Cat.
"And I will!" said the Little Mouse.

And together they ate up all of the breakfast, and it tasted oh, so good!
And from that time on, the Little Cat and the Little Mouse
have always helped the Little Red Hen.

RESOURCES

Florence White Williams, The Little Red Hen: An Old English Folktale *(New York: The Sallfield Publishing Company 1918), PDF available at The Project Gutenberg, gutenberg.org/ files/18735/18735-h/18735-h.htm.*

Rum-Ti-Pum-Pum

A FOLKTALE FROM INDIA ADAPTED BY AIME CHEVALIER AND MEG FISHER

ONCE UPON A TIME, two beautiful birds lived in a beautiful tree. They were very happy and they sang:

Doodle-oodle-oodle-oodle-doo!

One day the king of the land rode by on his elephant and heard the beautiful song.

"That song is so beautiful, I must take one of these birds back to my palace, so that I may hear it always." And so he did.

The bird left alone in the tree was very sad. She decided she must get her friend back.

So, she put on her armor, picked up her drum, and set off for the palace.

RUM-TI-PUM-PUM, RUM-TI-PUM-PUM!:

On the way she met a cat.

"Where are you going?" said the cat.

"I am going to the palace to rescue my friend. The king has taken her for her song."

"I'll go with you," said the cat. "He took my kittens!"

"Hop into my drum and come with me," said the bird.

RUM-TI-PUM-PUM, RUM-TI-PUM-PUM!

On the way they met some ants.

"Where are you going?" said the ants.

"I am going to the palace to rescue my friend. The king has taken her for her song."

"We'll go with you," said the ants. "The king and his elephant trampled our ant hill!"

"Hop into my drum and come with me," said the bird.

RUM-TI-PUM-PUM, RUM-TI-PUM-PUM!

On the way they met a stick.

"Where are you going?" asked the stick.

"I am going to the palace to rescue my friend. The king has taken her for her song."

"I'll go with you," said the stick. "The king's men chopped down my tree!"

"Hop into my drum and come with me," said the bird.

RUM-TI-PUM-PUM, RUM-TI-PUM-PUM!

And they came next to a river.

"Where are you going?" said the river.

"I am going to the palace to rescue my friend. The king has taken her for her song."

"I'll go with you," said the river. "The king and his men make muddy my waters!"

"Flow into my drum and come with me," said the bird.

RUM-TI-PUM-PUM, RUM-TI-PUM-PUM!

Well, by now the drum was very heavy, but the bird was strong, and she finally got to the palace.

WHY ARE YOU HERE? asked the king.

"I have come to rescue my friend," said the bird.

YOU MAY NOT HAVE HER! said the king.

I MUST HAVE HER BEAUTIFUL SONGS!

At this the bird began to beat her drum.

RUM-TI-PUM-PUM, RUM-TI-PUM-PUM!

Cat, cat, come out of my drum! Frighten the chickens one by one.

RUM-TI-PUM-PUM, RUM-TI-PUM-PUM!

Stick, stick, come out of my drum! Chase away the horses one by one.

RUM-TI-PUM-PUM, RUM-TI-PUM-PUM!

Ants, ants, come out of my drum! Tickle the trampling elephant.

RUM-TI-PUM-PUM, RUM-TI-PUM-PUM!

River, river, flow out of my drum! Flow around the room until the bed's undone!

RUM-TI-PUM-PUM, RUM-TI-PUM-PUM!

Well, the king was so amazed by this, that he gave the bird back to her friend.

The two beautiful birds flew back to their beautiful tree.

The stick, the ants, and the cat all returned to the forest.

The river flowed back between its banks.

And one day, the king, who missed the beautiful bird and its song, set out on a journey.

He crossed the river carefully so as not to muddy it.

He walked carefully through the forest, making sure to harm no one.

And when he came to the beautiful tree, he sat down at the bottom of it, and he listened and listened to the beautiful song.

And from that day on, he visited often. They were friends.

The Chief and His Two Daughters

A TALE FROM ZIMBABWE ADAPTED BY STEPHEN SPITALNY

This story originated from one told in the Shona language of Zimbabwe. In Shona, "Chipo" means gift, and "Chinangwa" means purpose or intention.

THERE WAS ONCE A VERY OLD MAN, and he had many cows, goats, donkeys, and plenty of land. With so much land, he grew plenty of food, enough to share with his neighbors. On top of all of that, he was a very wise man. He was the Chief of his village.

This Village Chief had two daughters. These daughters were twins, and he loved them both, one as much as the other. The twins were named Chipo and Chinangwa.

The Chief knew his own end was coming, and so he wanted to find out which daughter was the wisest, so that he could pass on his title as Village Chief before his own days were done. He called his two daughters together and spoke.

"Chipo and Chinangwa, my daughters," he said, "I love you both and I cannot choose who is the wiser of you. Before I go to join my ancestors, one of you must become Chief. I do not want to favor one or the other of you, and yet I have to choose which of you is the wisest.

"In our house there are two large rooms. They are exactly the same. What I want you to do, my daughters, is to each fill up one of the rooms. The room must be completely filled, side to side and top to bottom. In one week's time I will check to see which of you has completed this task."

Now, this was a hard job. What could you do to fill a room completely, and in one short week? This was a challenging test. He was indeed a wise Chief.

That night, the moon was shining and the two sisters went into the forest, each on her own way. They each spent the night in silent thought, until by dawn they knew what they would do.

Chinangwa came out of the forest in the morning and went back to their house.

Chipo went down to the river where there were many stones, and she began carrying some to the house. Back and forth she went, from river to the house and back again. By the end of the first day, she had made little progress. Early the next day she resumed carrying the rocks. She worked until the sun set, scarcely taking the time to eat and barely taking a rest. Each day she got to work early and didn't stop until dark.

At the end of the week Chipo was sad. Her father went and looked in her room and saw that it was only half full.

So he went to find Chinangwa.

Chinangwa had waited until the week had nearly passed, and on the last night she headed for her room with her hands holding only a few small items. All the people in the village thought she was crazy. How could she fill a room with just those few small items? Chinangwa ignored them and went quietly to her room.

The Chief followed her into the room. Everyone in the village came to watch through the windows. Chinangwa knelt down in the middle of the room and put a candle on a small dish. She took a match stick from her matchbox, struck it, and lit the candle. The whole room was filled with light, from floor to ceiling, from wall to wall. Chinangwa's candle filled the room with light. She had done it; the room was filled.

The old Chief could see that Chinangwa's wisdom shone brightly. When the old Chief died, Chinangwa was made the new Chief and she appointed her sister Chipo as First Advisor. They governed with wisdom and strength for many, many years.

The Snow Maiden

A RUSSIAN FOLKTALE TRANSLATED BY ANNA ANTONOVA

Anna translated this story based on a text collected by Alexander Afanasyev, a Russian historian and ethnographer who gathered nearly 600 Slavic folk and fairy tales, one of the largest collections of folklore in the world. She believes that this translation serves the archetypes and rhythm of the Russian language.

THE SUN ROSE, faint and soft as the days became shorter. Birds flew to the warm countries and forest animals stocked up on food in their burrows. From the northern mountains and arctic sea, a rider on a white horse came galloping. King Winter was his name. He covered all lands with a blanket of shining snow and turned rivers into crystalline ice.

An old man and old woman lived in a small hut on the edge of a village. They lived together peacefully, but they had a sorrow, for they had no children. King Winter made soft high snowdrifts and children of the village played joyfully, making snowmen, skating and skiing, laughing and singing. But the old man and the old woman watched them sadly through the frozen window, thinking about their sorrow.

"My dear, let's go outside and make for us a daughter out of snow," said the old man.

"Let's do it," answered the old woman.

They went to the yard and began to mold a snow girl. They made snowballs, fitted hands and legs and attached a head and they inserted blue beads for eyes and red berries for a mouth. The old man and old woman looked at and admired their Snow Maiden. Suddenly, she opened her eyes and smiled at them. She moved her hands and legs and shook snow from her coat. The Snow Maiden came alive from the snowdrift.

The old man and old woman's joy was so great that they brought the Snow Maiden into the hut, and looked at her and admired her. She lived with them and each day became prettier. But her cheeks stayed white as a snow. She was bright and smart, kind and merry. She helped her parents, did her chores easily and sang songs with delight.

Father Sun was brightening up his face, icicles dripped soundlessly, and the south wind brought a rider on a red horse. Beauty Spring was the red rider's name. Beauty Spring turned the grass green, opened snowdrop buds and let birds sing their cheering songs. But only Snow Maiden became sad and sorrowful.

The old man asked her, "What's happened to you? Why you are so sad? Maybe you are not feeling well?"

Snow Maiden answered, "Don't worry, Daddy, don't worry, Mommy. I'm feeling fine."

The last snow melted, flowers blossomed in meadows and thunder pounded in the sky, and a rider on a green horse came. Hot Summer was the green rider's name. But Snow Maiden became even sadder and more silent. She hid from Father Sun's rays in cool, shady spots. Once a dark cloud covered the sky and icy hail scattered on the ground. Snow Maiden was so delighted to see the hailstones; it was as if they were precious pearls. When Father Sun melted the icy hail, she cried bitterly, as if she had lost her own dear brother.

The day of the summer solstice came, and girls and boys gathered to go to the birch groove. They called Snow Maiden, "Come with us to sing and dance, rejoice and play on this summer day!"

Snow Maiden didn't want to go to the forest, but the old woman talked her into it, "Go, dear child, have cheer and joy with your friends!"

Snow Maiden went to the forest with her friends. They gathered flowers, wove wreaths of blossoms, sang songs, played and danced in a circle. Only Snow Maiden was still joyless and sad. At night, they brought brushwood and made a fire. Boys and girls jumped over the fire, holding hands. Snow Maiden was the last one, staying behind them.

In her turn she ran and jumped over the fire. Suddenly she melted away and turned into a white cloud. The white cloud rose higher and higher until it disappeared in the dark sky. Her friends heard a sad moaning behind them. "Auuu-Auuu!" They turned back and there was no Snow Maiden. They began to call her, but only an echo in the forest answered them. Snow Maiden flew over the high mountains, wide meadows and dark woods. She became a small cloud, a weightless veil, that rained down on the land the sweet rain and turned green fields to white with the blooming daisies.

Don't be sad, old man and old woman!

RESOURCES

Alexander Nikolayevich Afanasyev, Издательство: Современный писатель (*The Poetic Outlook of Slavs about Nature; Moscow: Modern Writer 1995*).

The Little, Small, Wee, Tiny Man

DIANA ROSS

This story was submitted by Lucy Wolf, who tells us, "Sandy Chamberlin gave me a xeroxed copy of "The Little Small Wee Tiny Man" when we were both students at Sunbridge College in 1997. Everything about this story appealed to me. I later found a copy of the book Nursery Tales *at Trinity College, Dublin, and read every story while sitting in an alcove of that college library.*

"Small children can relate to the little man. Adults, cow, dogs and other creatures often seem so much bigger than they are. The story also offers reverence for the smallest creatures— perfect for the springtime awakening of the natural world.

"One nursery occasion comes to mind: As the children poured outside after storytime, two went to step on the ants. Another child stopped them in their tracks, booming at them with the true voice of just authority: 'STOP!! One of them might be the little, small, wee, tiny ant!' "

ONCE UPON A TIME there was a little, small, wee, tiny man. *So* small, so very, very small. Why, he was only *so* big!

And he lived all alone in a little house, such a little, small, wee, tiny house it was. Why, his house was only *that* big.

And every day he went out and picked one grain of wheat and ground it up to make his loaf of bread. And he filled his bucket with one drop of dew, and one stewed blackberry gave him puddings for a week. And he had a good appetite for such a very little, small, wee, tiny man.

But he lived all alone and that made him very sad. And he cried and cried and *one, two, three, four, five!* Five little, small, wee, tiny tears fell from his eyes and rolled down his cheeks and splashed one, two, three, four, five, five little splashes on the floor.

So then it got to be known that the little, small, wee, tiny man was sad at living alone, and was sitting indoors all day crying and crying.

One day a child came to the place where the little, small, wee, tiny house was standing, and after looking round and about very hard, the child saw it and knelt down.

Now the child was *so* big, and therefore spoke very, very softly so as not to frighten the little, small, wee, tiny man.

"Little man, little man, shall I come and live with you?"

But though the child spoke so softly to the little, small, wee, tiny man, to him it sounded like this:

LITTLE MAN, LITTLE MAN, SHALL I COME LIVE WITH YOU?

And the little, small, wee, tiny man was so frightened, he ran and shut the door and shut all the windows and ran and crept under his little, small, wee, tiny bed and, putting his hands to his mouth, he cried out as loud as he could, "Go away, go away! You are MUCH too big."

But as loud as he shouted, all the child heard was a little, small, wee, tiny squeaking, like the voice of a mosquito: *eeeeeeeeeeeee!*

So the child got up and went away.

And the little, small, wee, tiny man came out from under his bed and began to cry. One, two, three, four, five little tears made one, two, three, four, five little splashes on the floor.

Next came a cat, who at once saw the little, small, wee, tiny house because, being a cat, her eyes were very sharp. She was a black cat and SO big.

And she said very softly, so as not to frighten the little, small, wee, tiny man:

"Miaow, miaow. Little man, little man, shall I come live with you?"

But though the cat spoke so softly, to the little, small, wee, tiny man, to him it sounded like this:

MIAOW, MIAOW. LITTLE MAN, LITTLE MAN, SHALL I COME AND LIVE WITH YOU?

And the little, small, wee, tiny man was so frightened, he ran to the window to see what this might be, and all he saw was a HUGE yellow eye, and it quite filled the whole window pane. So he pulled the curtains over the window and crept under his little, small, wee, tiny bed and put his hands to his mouth and shouted as the top of his voice:

"Go away, go away! You are MUCH too big."

But so loud as he shouted, all the cat could hear was a little, small, wee, tiny squeaking, like the voice of a mosquito: *eeeeeeeeeeee!*

So the cat got up and went away.

And the little, small, wee, tiny man came out from under the bed and began to cry. One, two, three, four, five little tears made one, two, three, four, five splashes on the floor.

Next there came a mouse, and a not very big mouse either, for she was only so big. And she did not take long to find the little house, for she smelled his bread baking in the oven. And up she went, sniff, sniff, sniffing at the door, and spoke very softly so as not to frighten the little, small, wee, tiny man.

"Squeak, squeak. Little man, little man, shall I come live with you?"

But softly though she spoke, to the little, small, wee, tiny man it sounded like this:

SQUEAK, SQUEAK, LITTLE MAN, LITTLE MAN, SHALL I COME LIVE WITH YOU?

And the little, small, wee, tiny man was so frightened he ran to the window to see what it might be, and he saw a huge, wet, grey, whiskery nose and it quite filled the whole window. He was so frightened that he shut the shutters and ran as quick as he could and crept under the bed and, putting his hands to his mouth, he shouted as loud as he could:

"Go away, go away! You are MUCH too big."

But so loud as he shouted, all the mouse could hear was a little, small, wee, tiny squeaking, like the voice of a mosquito: *eeeeeeeeeeee!*

So the mouse got up and went away.

And the little, small, wee, tiny man came out from under the bed and began to cry. One, two, three, four, five little tears made one, two, three, four, five little splashes on the floor.

But now there came an ant, and when she saw the little, small, wee, tiny house she said to herself, "Oh my, oh my, what a very fine gentleman he must be to live in such a fine big house."

And she went to the door and rang the bell rather timidly—*ting, ting, ting.*

And the little, small, wee, tiny man went to the door and opened it. There he saw the ant, and such a nice, little, small, wee, tiny creature she looked, with her shiny red skin and her pretty little legs and her tiny waving antennae, that he liked her at once.

And when she said in a clear voice: "Good sir, I hope you will not think me too bold if I suggest coming to live with you," it sounded to him just like this:

"Good sir, I hope you will not think me too bold if I suggest coming to live with you."

He answered at once, "Oh, you lovely little creature, come in, come in. I have been so sad all alone in my little, small, wee, tiny house. But if you will come and live with me, why, then we can both be happy from morning till night."

And the ant went in and ran all over the house and thought it the very grandest place she had ever been in.

So ever after that, the little, small, wee, tiny man picked *two* grains of wheat every day and made *two* little loaves for himself and the ant. And he went *twice* and filled his little bucket with *two* drops of dew, and as for the pudding, he had to pick *two* big blackberries instead of only one, for the ant was very fond of her pudding and ate it all up every day.

So the little, small, wee, tiny man never again shed one, two, three, four, five little tears, but lived happily ever after with the even smaller, wee-er, tinier, extremely little ant!

RESOURCES

Diana Ross, Nursery Tales *(London: Faber and Faber 1969).*

The Rolling Pumpkin

A PERSIAN FOLKTALE ADAPTED BY JENNY TAYLOR

This story has been adapted from its written form for telling aloud in the early childhood classroom. It works very well as a puppet show "in the round"—the puppeteer is at the center of the circle of children, and puppets move around the circle as the story is told.

ONCE UPON A TIME, an old grandmother wanted to visit her daughter on the other side of the woods. Now, it was dark in the woods, and a little scary, so when a big wolf jumped out into the path ahead of her, Grandma was startled.

"Don't be afraid, Grandma," said the wolf. "I only want to ask where you are going."

"I'm going to visit my daughter on the other side of the woods," said Grandma. "I'd be pleased if you would let me pass."

"Surely," said the wolf, "but first you must promise to bring me some candy and cookies from your daughter's house when you return. Lots and lots of candy and cookies." The wolf licked his chops.

Grandma promised, the wolf stepped back, and she hurried on her way. She hadn't gone far when a big bear jumped out into the path ahead of her.

"Don't be afraid, Grandma," said the bear. "I only want to ask where you are going."

"I'm going to visit my daughter on the other side of the woods," said Grandma. "I'd be pleased if you would let me pass."

"Surely," said the bear, "but first you must promise to bring me some nice honey from your daughter's house when you return. Lots and lots of honey." The bear licked his chops.

Grandma promised, the bear stepped back, and she hurried on her way. She had not gone far when a lion jumped out and stood in the path ahead of her.

"Don't be afraid, Grandma," said the lion. "I only want to ask where you are going."

"I'm going to visit my daughter on the other side of the woods," said Grandma. "I'd be pleased if you would let me pass."

"Surely," said the lion. "but first you must promise to bring me some meat from your daughter's house. Lots and lots of meat." The lion licked his chops.

Grandma promised, the lion stepped back, and she hurried on her way.

When Grandma reached her daughter's house, she was quite out of breath and now a little worried. She told her daughter everything.

"What shall I do?" she exclaimed. "Even if you had all those things, which you don't, I should have to carry them, which I can't."

They sat for a time, drinking tea and talking, and thinking. Then the daughter had an idea. "I have a giant pumpkin in my garden," she said. "I will hollow it out, put you in it, and roll you down the path through the woods. Since it is downhill all the way, you can roll right home."

"What a good idea!" said Grandma. And that is what they did. Grandma and her daughter set to work carving the pumpkin, and presently she was on her way through the woods, safe inside the rolling pumpkin. When she came to the lion, he called out,

Stop, Pumpkin, Rolling Pumpkin! Have you seen Grandma?

From inside the pumpkin, Grandma called out,

I cannot stop, I must not stay, I saw no Grandma going this way.

And on she rolled. She hadn't gone far when she met the bear, who called out,

Stop, Pumpkin, Rolling Pumpkin! Have you seen Grandma?

From inside the pumpkin, Grandma called,

I cannot stop, I must not stay, I saw no Grandma going this way.

And on she rolled. She hadn't gone far when she met the wolf, who called out,

Stop, Pumpkin, Rolling Pumpkin! Have you seen Grandma?

From inside the pumpkin, Grandma called out,

I cannot stop, I must not stay, I saw no Grandma going this way.

But the wolf decided to stop that pumpkin anyway. He gave a mighty leap, landed on top of it, and broke it open. To his surprise, out jumped Grandma. Quick as a wink she ran home and slammed the door.

As for the wolf and his greedy friends the bear and the lion, they had to content themselves with eating pumpkin. Lots and lots of pumpkin.

RESOURCES

From Ladybug: the Magazine for Young Children, *October 2013 (McLean, Virginia: Cricket Media), retold by Marilyn Bolchunis.*

The Old Woman by the Sea

A FOLKTALE FROM CHILE ADAPTED BY LOUISE deFOREST

Long ago there was an old woman who lived in a tumble-down shack by the sea.

The sea was like a mother to her. It brought her fish to eat and wood to burn, and it sang to her day and night. But when it was stormy, the old woman was afraid because she knew that deep in the sea caves and underwater forests there hid hungry sea-wolves, waiting for a storm.

The village children were all afraid of the old woman who lived in the tumble-down shack and who walked the shore every day. When they saw her, they made faces at her behind her back, but when she turned around, they fled. How the old woman longed for the children to be her friends!

One day a storm came, and it was terrible. The winds shook the hut and tore at the roof. The sea-wolves threw back their heads and howled and then out they came. All night they prowled the shore, howling and baying in the wind and rain. All night the old woman trembled in the corner of her shed.

When dawn came, the winds tired and the sea-wolves crept back into their caves. The old woman opened her door and looked out. The storm had blown the sky clear of clouds and the sunlight smiled down at the shore.

She stood in the warm sunlight to warm her rickety-rackety bones and looked around. Taking up her gathering basket, the old woman walked along the shore.

"The sea has brought me fish and wood!" she said to herself as she filled her basket.

She came upon a rock pool, and when she peered into its clear waters she saw the largest crab she had ever seen.

"There's enough crab here to feed me all week!" she thought, and she put the crab into her basket.

When her basket was so full she could hardly lift it, she struggled back to her hut and placed it on her table. She saw that the crab shell had opened. And she saw something else.

"Why, what is this?" she exclaimed. It was a baby girl, with hair the color of the setting sun, skin like a rosy pearl, and a fish's tail with scales of silver.

"Look what the sea has brought me!" cried the old woman, and she was happier than she had ever been.

She carried the baby in her crab shell cradle to the village, went straight to the house of the Wise Woman, and placed the child in her arms.

For a long time, the Wise Woman gazed at the child and said nothing. Then she said, "This is a Merbaby. Her mother hid her in the crab shell to keep her safe from the sea-wolves."

"Then I must let the mother know she is safe," said the old woman. "Who is her mother?"

"A Sea Spirit," said the Wise Woman. "Put the Merbaby safely on a rock out of reach of the sea-wolves and her mother will find her."

The old woman returned to the shore and placed the crab shell high on a rock. She smiled down at the child and said, "You're not afraid of me, are you?" And the baby just smiled at her.

The old woman hid herself and waited. She waited a long time. She was almost asleep when she heard someone singing, but not words from this world.

Seven great waves came rolling into shore and on the seventh wave rode the Sea Spirit. She was as tall as the mast of a great ship. Her hair was as red as the setting sun and her skin was as smooth and as white as a pearl. All the colors of the rainbow shimmered in her tail. She looked towards the shore and saw the crab shell, high on a rock.

The Sea Spirit picked up the Merbaby and sang a lullaby to her, a song not of this world. Her voice was like the murmur of the sea on a calm day.

"I did not mean to take your baby," cried the old woman when she saw the Sea Spirit. "I thought she was a gift from the sea."

The Sea Spirit looked at the old woman and smiled. "The sea did bring her to you, old woman. I hid her inside the shell to keep her from the sea-wolves, but the storm swept the cradle away and brought her to you. You have saved her life. Look after her for me. I will come every day to feed her and teach her how to swim."

So, the old woman and the Merchild lived together in the tumble-down hut, safe from the restless sea. They were very poor, but the sea brought them all that they needed, and they were very happy.

The Merchild grew stronger and taller and her hair grew longer. She liked to lie in the shallow waves and watch the village children. The village children came closer and closer, and they no longer ran away when the old woman smiled at them.

The Merchild learned to speak the words of our world. When she sang, her voice was like the echo of the sea inside a shell.

Each day the Sea Spirit rode in on the seventh wave. She fed the Merchild and taught her to swim in the sheltered rock pool, and then further out at sea.

As the old woman watched the Sea Spirit and the Merchild dancing on the waves she grew very sad. "How I dread the time when you will go back to the sea, little Merchild," she said to herself. She thought of keeping the child locked in her hut so the Sea Spirit could not take her away. "No," thought the old woman, "The Merchild is from the sea and to the sea she must return. I must let her go."

But the Merchild stayed with the old woman for many more days. Now the village children filled the old woman's hut. The Merchild would make them necklaces of shells and the old woman would cook them food, and everyone would sit together to share the gifts from the sea.

At last the morning came that the old woman was dreading. The Sea Spirit sang, "My child can swim now and it is time to take her home. The sea is calm and the sea-wolves cannot catch her. But we will never forget you, old woman." And she took the Merchild on her back, far, far out to sea while the old woman watched from the shore, tears falling down her face.

The children came up behind the old woman and took her hands and comforted her.

But the Merchild had not gone forever. Each morning she leaped from the waves to greet the old woman and send her a beautiful pearl from the sea-bed. The Sea Spirit always sent waves brimful of fish. When there was a storm, the sea-wolves still howled, but the old woman was no longer afraid for she knew she was watched over by the Sea-Spirit and her child.

And so they did, all the days of her life.

RESOURCES

Caroline Pitcher, Mariana and the Merchild: a Folktale from Chile *(Grand Rapids, Michigan 2000).*

The Hen and the King

A SPANISH TALE ADAPTED BY LOUISE deFOREST

ONCE UPON A TIME there was a little hen, and she was as white as snow. She had a comb on her head of purest gold and it shone like the sun at midday. And, indeed, the hen was exceedingly proud of her beauty and believed she was fit to be the wife of none other than the king.

One fine day she was pecking away at a heap of dust and she found a diamond. It was a big one, a giant one, and shone a hundred times stronger than the sun itself. When the hen saw it, she thought happily:

"I shall take it to the royal palace. I shall give it to the king, and when the king sees me he will immediately fall in love with me and make me his wife."

So she fashioned a basket of grass, just a small one, yet it was very dainty and charming. She hung the basket round her neck, placed the diamond in it, and set off for the royal palace.

When the other animals saw the hen setting off on her journey, with her comb glistening like pure gold, they ran out to look at her, asking:

> *"Whither, little hen, are you hurrying so,*
> *With crest a-glitter, like sun on snow?"*

And the little hen proudly replied:

> *"I'm off to the palace to marry the king;*
> *I'll give him this jewel for his wedding ring."*

And each and every animal bowed respectfully to the little hen and wished her a pleasant journey and good luck in her undertaking. They hoped that she would soon be queen, each and every one of them, except the wicked wolf. He ran out from the deep forest, where even the daytime it is as dark as the night, and he planted himself in the middle of the path and shouted in a harsh voice:

> *"Whither, little hen, are you hurrying so,*
> *Looking as ugly as Jack the Crow?"*

But the little hen replied politely:

> *"I'm off to the palace to marry the king;*
> *I'll give him this jewel for his wedding ring."*

To which the wolf howled in an even harsher voice:

> *"You won't get married, I tell you true,*
> *For here and now I'll devour you!"*

But the little hen quickly pulled the diamond from the basket with her beak and showed it to the wolf. No sooner did he see it, than the wolf began to get smaller and smaller, till he was no bigger than a flea. Whereupon the little hen caught him in her beak, put him into the basket and walked on.

On the way through the forest she came to a large tree, so tall that its branches reached the sky, so great in girth that not even a hundred men could encompass it with their arms. It was the king of the oaks. It stood in the hen's way and shouted with a voice of thunder:

"Whither, little hen, are you hurrying so,
Looking as ugly as Jack the Crow?"

But the little hen replied politely:

"I'm off to the palace to marry the king;
I'll give him this jewel for his wedding ring."

To which the oak rumbled out even louder than before:

"You won't get married, I tell you true,
For I am going to fall on you!"

But the little hen quickly pulled the diamond from the basket with her beak and showed it to the king of oaks. No sooner did it see it, than that oak began to grow smaller and smaller and smaller, till it was no bigger than a blade of grass. Whereupon the little hen picked it up in her beak and put it into the basket and journeyed on. On her way she came to a great rushing river, and there was neither ferry nor bridge across it. The little hen stopped and said:

"River, dear river, flowing so fast,
Halt for a moment till I have passed."

Whereupon the river grew more turbulent than ever and said:

"Not for a moment, as you should know,
Can I arrest this mighty flow.
I must keep driving down to the sea,
For there the tides are waiting for me."

But the little hen pulled the diamond from the basket and showed it to the water. No sooner had the river seen it, then it began to get smaller and smaller, smaller and smaller, till it was no bigger than a drop of dew. This the hen picked up in her beak and placed in the basket, and she journeyed on again toward the royal palace.

She went on and on, for seven days and seven nights, without a rest, until she came to the royal palace. Here she was stopped by a guard, who said he would not let her pass. But the little hen just pulled out the diamond and showed it to him, saying:

> *"I've come to the palace to marry the king;*
> *I'll give him this jewel for his wedding ring."*

And the guard immediately let her through. In the middle of the royal suite the little hen met the king's steward. He wasn't much impressed with her feathers, as white and spotless as new fallen snow, nor with her little crest of gold. In fact, he thought that one of the king's hens must have escaped from the yard. He ordered a servant to catch her and put her back in the chicken coop. But the little hen stepped up boldly to him and said:

> *"I've come to the palace to marry the king;*
> *I'll give him this jewel for his wedding ring."*

The steward took the diamond from the little hen and carried it to the king, and the king said, "Who sent this to me?"

"A funny little hen, your majesty," answered the steward.

"Tell her I am very grateful, and then put her back in the chicken coop where she belongs."

And so the servants seized the little hen and pushed her into the chicken coop. There all the cocks and hens attacked her roughly with their beaks. Then the little hen remembered the wolf and called out:

> *"Little wolf, keep me safe from harm*
> *And I'll release you from the charm."*

Whereupon the wolf jumped out of the basket and in an instant was as large as before and hurled himself on the cocks and hens. In less than no time he had disposed of them all, except the little hen with the golden comb.

The day had scarcely dawned when the little hen ran to the palace and began strutting up and down the splendid royal suite. When the servants saw her, they ran to tell the king that the little hen had escaped from the chicken coop.

The king was very angry and said, "For this insolence, throw her into jail!" So the servants again caught the little hen and threw her into the deepest dungeon.

The dungeon had walls as thick and strong as seven carriages standing side by side. It was so narrow that the little hen could scarcely move and so dark that it was like everlasting night there. The little hen almost suffocated. Then she tipped the blade of grass from the basket and said:

"Mighty oak grow tall and straight!
Save me from this fearful fate!"

And the oak took root and began to grow so quickly that in the twinkling of an eye it was taller than the tallest tower. It knocked down the prison walls, and half the palace as well.

When the king heard what had happened, he was beside himself with rage and ordered the little hen to be thrown into the oven. One was already prepared, because the cooks were about to bake a cake for the king's breakfast.

The servants seized the little hen and thrust her into the hot oven. But the little hen shook the drop of water from her basket and said:

"River, keep me safe from harm
And I'll release you from the charm."

And immediately the drop of water began to swell and became a torrent, putting out the oven fire and flooding the whole palace. It knocked down all that stood in its way and carried everything to the sea.

The king only just got away with his life. And as he saw that he could not overpower the little hen with the golden comb, he thought he had better marry her instead.

Their wedding was royal and festive and they lived together for many a long year in peace and contentment. They had children by the score, because the little hen laid an egg every single day, and all their children became kings and queens.

RESOURCES

Vladislav Stanovsky and Jan Vladislav, The Fairy Tale Tree *(New York: G.P. Putnam's Sons 1961).*

Dragon Pearls

A STORY FROM CHINA ADAPTED BY STEPHEN SPITALNY

ONCE UPON A TIME, a brother and a sister lived together on the edge of a small village near the forest. Their parents had died and the two children worked very hard so they could get enough food to live by. They tended their garden and were kind to all the animals of the forest.

One winter, brother grew very ill and no one was able to help him, no doctors could cure him. He lay in the bed and could scarcely sit up.

Not long after, the sister was working alone in their garden, and a wise and kind old woman came along. She told the sister about a dragon who lives high in the mountains who helps people in need, and who might be able to help her brother.

The girl left her brother in the care of the kind old woman and set out to find the dragon. She wandered for a long time, through fields and meadows, and up into the mountains.

> Across the meadows
> Across the fields
> Climbing up the mountain, way up high
> Please help my brother.
> Please help my brother.
> I won't go home, I must try and try.

She eventually came to a cave which was surrounded by jasmine bushes of amazing beauty and scent. There she found the dragon.

The girl told the dragon about her brother and the dragon promised to help her. The dragon said she would find the cure.

The dragon leaped up and soared high into the sky. The girl could see the beautiful pearls around the dragon's neck, glittering in the sun. The dragon flew back to the girl and then opened her jaws. A large seed fell from her mouth and onto the ground, and a beautiful tea bush sprouted and started immediately growing. The dragon told the girl to take good care of the tea bush, and then she disappeared, leaving the girl alone at the cave.

It rained hard that season but the girl looked after the tea bush, not leaving its side even for a moment. She made sure the rain did not flood the young bush. She stayed when the sun shone brightly and made sure the tea bush got enough water. And the tea bush grew. And grew.

When spring came, small, long leaves appeared. The girl gathered the most delicate leaves from the end of each branch, and dried them alongside the jasmine flowers. When the leaves were dry, she made delicate beads out of the tea leaves and jasmine flowers. They looked just like the pearls that hung around the neck of the dragon. She filled her basket with the dragon pearl tea balls she had made.

Then she took the long journey to return to her home. When she arrived, she brewed some of the dragon pearls. Their house was filled with a wonderful aroma. Her brother sat up when he smelled the delicious aroma. When he drank some of the delicious tea his sister brewed, he quickly recovered, and he was stronger and healthier than ever.

Brother and Sister thanked the old woman, and the old woman returned to her home. And Brother and Sister lived happy and healthy lives for a very long time.

Farmer Pete's Pumpkin Patch

SUSAN STARR

Susan offers this story, which she uses as a puppet play, in memory of Peter Dukich, a biodynamic farmer and the Johnny Appleseed of composting.

ETWEEN TWO HIGH MOUNTAINS, where a river once flowed wide, there was a narrow valley. Farmer Pete and his wife came to live in the lowland valley and made their little farm there. Farmer Pete used to go out at night and watch the stars and he saw so many stars shining that he would often say to his wife, "So many children are coming down from the land of stars. We must make the earth sweet and grow fresh food for the star children coming down the rainbow bridge." They knew that the children played their best when they had good food, so for many days they worked to make the soil rich and sweet.

Farmer Pete always left a little part of the farm for the wild animals that came to graze there. The animals were grateful for his kindness and never ate the vegetables in his garden.

Every autumn he made a fresh "Mother Earth Cake," which is what he called a compost pile. He raked all the autumn leaves and piled them into a tall pile. He added kitchen scraps and weeds pulled from his garden. When his Mother Earth Cake was complete, he covered it with golden straw to protect it and keep it warm through the cold months ahead. Father Sun's autumn rays kept the cake very warm; Sister Rain made it moist and Brother Wind happily flew over the Mother Earth Cake and was very careful to not let Jack Frost freeze it on a cold autumn night.

When spring planting season came to the valley, Farmer Pete opened up his Mother Earth Cake and began to spread some of the compost over his land and to rake it in. Then he began his planting.

Add a planting song here, if you like.

Father Sun climbed higher in the sky and helped the seeds to sprout and grow while Sister Rain made the soil soft and moist. Each day Farmer Pete's corn grew higher and higher, and his pumpkin patch grew wider and wider with orange-colored blossoms turning to round orange balls.

The farm now had new spring chicks. While Farmer Pete tended the farm, Farmer Pete's wife took care of the chickens and tended her roses.

One autumn night, when the corn was high and almost ready for harvest, and the pumpkins were ready for the children to come and pick them and turn them into jack-o-lanterns, Farmer Pete went out and saw the frost gathering on the mountain tops. He called up to the stars and said, "Please do not let the silver frost come down to the valley floor. The children will be sad not to have their pumpkins firm and the vines fresh and green. The frost will turn the corn all hard."

But each night as he went out, the frost came lower and lower. One evening just as the sun was setting, he called up to Father Sun and asked him to leave a golden ray over the valley so that Jack Frost would not come too near. Then he commended himself to his evening thoughts and went to bed.

Not long afterwards, from over the crest where the last golden ray touched the mountain, came the wise stag with the golden horn.

Add appropriate music here, if you wish.

Down, down, down the stag descended to the valley floor. He bent and sniffed the earth. The soil always tells the wild creatures what humans are doing, and here he could smell that Farmer Pete cared for the land that grew his food. He also visited the pumpkin patch and walked so carefully that he did not break even one tender vine. Then the wise stag with the golden horn ascended the mountain and all night long breathed his warm breath along the frost line so that it could not come down into the valley.

When Father Sun's morning rays touched the valley floor, Farmer Pete came out to see if any plants were spared from the frost. As he walked the fields, he saw the tracks of a large stag, but nothing had been eaten or harmed.

Soon the farm was open for picking pumpkins from the pumpkin patch. The children gleefully arrived and ran through the corn fields. Then they went to pick their pumpkins to take home for making jack-o-lanterns. It was a splendid autumn day.

As the sun was setting, Farmer Pete and his wife looked up to the heavenly sky and wondered at how Jack Frost had spared their farm. Looking up to the high mountain, they knew that the nature spirits had sent them a helper.

Minka and Twilight

MINDY UPTON

Mindy was inspired by Mongolian felted puppets and Mongolian story culture to create this story, which she presents as a puppet play.

FAR AWAY BUT NOT TOO LONG AGO, there was a family of nomads who lived simply and happily in the plains of their beautiful country in Mongolia. Deep in the folds of a valley where mountains grew through the clouds and the horses and cattle roamed freely, Minka lived with his family—Momma, Poppa, and Big Sister. Minka helped his Poppa and Momma build their house made of wool. Their round house, a yurt, had thick, woolen walls that kept the warmth of the fires inside all winter long. Minka and Big Sister had a small bed that was covered with many-colored blankets and furs. A small, covered window was right next to Minka's bed. So, in the morning, Minka could be the first to see the sun on the horizon; and in the evening, he could see the moon rise from the mountain top before he went to sleep.

Simmering butter tea was served from the fire in the morning to start off the day when the rooster reminded them that morning had come. It was now time to tend to their animals and do the day's chores.

After slowly putting on his layers of woolen shirts, coat, boots, and mittens, off Minka would go to do what he always would do . . . watch. He would watch as Poppa gathered the oats for the horses. He would watch as Momma gathered corn for the chickens, and he would watch as Big Sister started to walk over to her favorite spot to call in the horses. This was Minka's favorite part of the day. Minka would sit and watch as the horses heard Big Sister's sweet whistle-song in the cold air.

The rumble and roar of the horses' hooves would begin to shake the earth. All the horses would come running, led by the strongest, fastest horse in the world. At least this was what Minka thought. This magnificent white horse was named Twilight. When Twilight came close, he would always stop for a moment and turn his head to Minka as if to say, "Come with me." Minka would sit and look at Twilight in awe.

Minka would watch as Big Sister greeted the horses and served them their daily meal. Then she would gather her blanket and saddle to go for her daily ride. She first put on the blanket, then the leather saddle. "Come on, Minka!" she would call. "Come and ride!"

But Minka would just shake his head and watch as Big Sister jumped on top of Twilight and started to ride. Off they would go into the brilliance of the morning light twinkling on Twilight and Big Sister. Twilight ran as if he had wings on his hooves. They hardly touched the ground. His mane danced in Big Sister's face as the golden dust from the ground flew to make clouds on the earth. Oh, how Minka longed to ride, too.

Every day he sat and watched and watched and watched. Every day a small carrot was in his pocket, just in case he got close enough to offer it. Just in case he decided that yes, he could ride too.

Every day Big Sister would call out, "Minka, come and ride!"

Every day Minka would sit and wait and watch.

"Minka, come! Minka, come and I will help you!" cried Big Sister.

Minka would just watch.

Night fell and Momma called everyone in for the night. After a day of feeding the animals, tending to the crops and riding the horses, everyone ate heartily and then readied for bed. Minka ate his soup, changed to his bedclothes, and took a bit of carrot which he placed by the window. "Maybe," he thought, "maybe he will come tonight. Maybe."

This night seemed different from other winter nights. The moon was as big as the sky. The sun was so far away. The cold breeze stopped. The snow on the mountain twinkled with silver. The stars sparked a brilliant light through the cold, frosty air. Minka's eyes felt heavy and he snuggled into his blanket and fell asleep.

Later, lying in bed, warm and cozy next to Big Sister, Minka heard a sound of crunching, munching. And there he was! There was Twilight, nibbling on his carrot!

Minka reached out to touch his warm nose. . . .

Twilight nuzzled the window with his nose and made the window turn warm. Twilight looked straight into Minka's eyes as if to say, "Minka, come and ride! Minka, come and ride! Minka, come and ride and I will help."

Minka looked into Twilight's eyes and deep within himself felt a feeling that he had never felt before. . .

"Yes . . ." Minka felt, "Yes!"

"Cock-a-doodle-doo!" Was it morning already? Minka looked out the window. The carrot was gone!

Butter tea was served as it always was with hugs and morning kisses, then layers of clothes. Minka couldn't wait to get outside to see the horses. He never got dressed so fast!

"Where are you going?" asked Big Sister.

"To see Twilight!"

Big Sister ran after Minka as fast as she could. She whistled and there they came—the entire herd, headed by Twilight. This time Minka gathered the blankets, the saddle, and the carrots, and stood and waited for Twilight.

Twilight stopped and stood patiently. Minka knew exactly what to do. He fastened the saddle just as he had seen Big Sister do, and then Twilight did exactly what he said he would do at the window last night: he bent down on his knees and helped Minka get up on his back.

Big Sister watched, Momma watched, Poppa watched. Minka was on top of Twilight! Twilight gave out a big "NEIGH!" and off the two went into the plains, galloping steadily. And the wind sang upon Minka's face.

The Secret Prince

DIANE VAN DOMMELEN

For an older group of children, especially only children or first-borns.

THERE WAS ONCE A PRINCESS who fell in love with a woodcutter. Though the king and queen wished that she would marry a prince, in their wisdom, they knew that true love could not be denied. The princess did not wish to carry her riches with her into her new life, and so only accepted a few jewels to be set aside for her children.

The princess and the woodcutter lived in a warm and cozy house at the edge of the forest in which the woodcutter worked. Theirs was a life filled with great love. They were blessed with a family of happy children, none of whom were told that their mother had been raised a princess before she became the wife of a woodcutter.

The time came for the two oldest children, a boy and a girl, to set out into the world to find their own paths to happiness. Their mother packed a bag for each of them, adding to each a hat, a pair of mittens, and a pair of socks that she had knitted herself; and some bread, cheese and fruit. In the bottom of each bag, she placed one of the precious jewels that she had saved, wrapped in a piece of cloth. Of these she did not tell her children when she placed the bags on their backs and hugged them farewell.

They decided to follow the path that led away from the forest, going whichever way it pleased them. It wasn't long before they came upon an old grandma and grandpa gathering sticks at the side of the road to take home and place on their fire. Their hands were red and cold. Being a robust young man with a good heart, the brother immediately opened his bag and removed the mittens that his mother had made and gave them to the old folks, who smiled in gratitude. But upon seeing this, the sister only closed her bag a little tighter and continued down the road.

Farther along, coming towards them, the brother and sister saw a father returning to his family from a faraway country. He was limping, for his stockings were in rags and his feet were blistered.

Once again, while the sister walked on, averting her eyes from the man, the brother stopped and opened his bag. He brought out the socks from his mother. "My own socks are still thick and strong," he thought. "This man needs these now more than I do." And he gave the footsore traveler the socks. The man accepted them gratefully and all continued their journeys.

The road led eventually to a castle wall. The gate was open, revealing a busy village and the great castle beyond. A tree stood beside the gate. Beneath it huddled two little children, a brother and sister like the older two themselves, shivering in the cold wind. They had no hats to warm their ears.

"We will be able to find new hats when we need them," said the brother to his sister. "Let us give our extra hats now to these little ones." But, even as the brother opened his bag, removed the hat his mother had knitted, and handed it to the children, the sister only held her own bag tightly to her chest.

What a bustle the village was in! When the sister and brother arrived at the castle, they understood why: That evening there was to be a ball! And all the young people, rich and poor, were invited to attend! Oh! Now the sister's eyes did sparkle!

"But, dear sister," said the brother, "We are not prepared to attend a ball. All we have to wear are the clothes on our backs."

"I must go to the ball," demanded the sister. "There is nothing I want more than to be a princess, for a princess never needs to share her riches with anyone!" And she burst into tears.

Seeing his sister's sorrow touched the brother's heart, and he reached into his bag to see if he had anything left that might make her feel better, a piece of cheese or morsel of dried apple. As he searched he felt something hard in the bottom of his bag. As he pulled it out of the bag, the wrapping fell away from the jewel and it lay in his hand, sparkling in the sun. He reached his hand out to his sister to show her the wonder.

Immediately, she grabbed the jewel from his palm.

"Hurry," he said. "Perhaps there is still time to find a dress to wear to the ball."

With only a glance his way, she turned and ran. Only after the sister had disappeared into the throng of the village did the brother notice her bag, thrown away in her haste to spend the jewel. He left it outside the gate on the chance she would return to look for it.

Now, whether his sister found a dress and went to the ball, or whether she indeed convinced a prince to marry her and make her a princess, we do not know. For this is the story of the brother.

As soon as he lost sight of his sister, with his now truly empty bag over his shoulder, the oldest son of the princess and the woodcutter went into the village. He found work with a baker, who happened to have a beautiful daughter. When they fell in love and wanted to marry, the baker gave them both his blessing and they built a little cottage at the edge of a forest.

There, they raised a happy and loving family.

Perhaps, they are living there still.

And though his mother never told him that he was the secret son of a princess, we know, do we not, that the son of the princess and the woodcutter was, and always will be, a true prince.

The Sarimanok and the Secret Garden

A STORY FROM THE PHILIPPINES
ADAPTED BY DEBORA PETSCHEK

ONCE UPON A TIME, in a sunny island far, far away, there lived a fisherman and his wife. They had a beautiful daughter named Haliya. They enjoyed many happy years together, living on fish and the bounty of the land. Then, one day, Haliya's mother took ill suddenly and died. With much sorrow in their hearts, they buried her in the cool shade of the nearby forest. Not long after, the fisherman met a widow with two daughters, and married her.

The stepmother was jealous of Haliya's beauty and kindness and determined to make her life miserable. The fisherman was gone for long periods of time, fishing for enough food to feed his large family. In his absence, the stepmother began treating Haliya cruelly, making her work from morning to night, cleaning the house, fetching water from the river, cooking all the meals, and tending the stove. All the while her stepsisters taunted her, calling her "Kitchen Princess." She was given no rest, and every night she would fall asleep on the kitchen floor, exhausted and sooty from her day's work.

One morning the stepmother came to Haliya and threw two handkerchiefs at her feet, saying: "Wash these two handkerchiefs until the white one turns black and the black one turns white! If you do not do as I say, it shall not go well for you!"

Crying sorrowfully, Haliya went to the riverbank and, not knowing what else to do, began to sing:

Mother, oh Mother Bathala, creator of the earth
Spirits of my ancestors, hear me and help me please

She heard the wind softly rustle the leaves of the trees, and there stood a beautiful woman bathed in radiant light. Her face was full of kindness. She said, "I am the Spirit of the Forest, guardian of all that lives and grows here. I have come because I heard your cry for help."

Gently, she took the two handkerchiefs and waved them in the air. Out of nowhere, two more spirits appeared. Each took a handkerchief and began a magical dance. With the handkerchiefs tossing about, they went round and round. When they stopped and handed the handkerchiefs back, Haliya saw that the white one was now black and the black one was now white. She hurried home to give them to her stepmother, who was not happy to see that she had accomplished the task.

The next morning, the stepmother ordered Haliya to spread rice on a mat in the sun to dry, and then pound, winnow, and cook it for the evening meal. While Haliya was busy in the kitchen, a pig wandered into the yard and gobbled up the drying rice, tearing the mat to tatters. The stepmother watched until the pig left, then ordered Haliya to weave the ruined mat into one whole piece again. With tears in her eyes, Haliya carried the mat to the river, where she sang Mother Bathala's song.

The Spirit of the Forest appeared and clapped her hands three times. A group of young spirits appeared and started to weave the mat back together. In a short time they handed back the mat, fully woven again. Before Haliya could thank them, the Spirit of the Forest gave her a Sarimanok, a beautiful jungle chicken with a long flowing tail and feathers the color of the rainbow. "Take this with you. It is now yours," she said.

When she arrived back at home, her stepmother was very angry to see the repaired mat. So early the next morning, while Haliya was busy elsewhere, she snuck into the coop, took the Sarimanok and slaughtered it for their dinner, leaving only the feet behind. When she discovered her pet bird was gone, Haliya gathered the feet and ran weeping to the river. The Spirit of the Forest was waiting for her. She told Haliya to bury the Sarimanok's feet by her mother's grave and pray to her ancestors. This she did, planting a garden around the burial mound. Then she began to pray, pouring her heart out to her mother "Dearest mother, since you left, the days are longer, the work is harder, and my tears flow like a river. Please touch my heart and give me strength."

In answer, a warm, gentle rain began to fall, washing away her tears and giving her comfort and strength.

Some time later, when Haliya next visited her mother's grave, she discovered that an enchanted tree had grown over the spot where she had buried the Sarimanok's feet. The tree was laden with treasures: rings, bracelets, necklaces, earrings, pearls, diamonds and golden gowns all hung from the boughs. Haliya decided to keep the tree a secret, and only took a few of the treasures with her, hiding them well, before returning to her piles of work.

Not long after, the son of the island chieftain was hunting in the forest, when he saw a Sarimanok. He followed it to Haliya's secret garden. There he caught sight of the tree. Realizing it was magic, he paid his respects to it by offering gifts. Kneeling before it, he prayed to Bathala: "Spirit of the Forest, please accept my gifts and allow me to receive one of your precious treasures." The prince picked a ring from a branch and slipped it onto his finger.

That evening, the prince's finger began to swell and he could not get the ring off. In great pain, he fell into a restless sleep and dreamt. In this dream, the Sarimanok came to him with an orchid in its beak. The prince took the flower and kissed it. It turned into a beautiful maiden. When she opened her hands, she was holding the ring and when he looked down, he saw it was no longer on his finger.

When the prince awoke, he went to his father and told him what he had dreamt. The chief, who was a wise man, summoned the island messenger and ordered, "Beat your drums! Tell everyone that the girl who can remove the ring from my son's finger shall be his bride!"

The news spread quickly and soon young women from all over the island were flocking to the chieftain's house, but none of them could remove the ring. When the news reached Haliya's house, she begged for permission to go, but her stepmother refused. She locked her in the house and lay down in a hammock just outside the door to sleep.

The Spirit of the Forest appeared and unlocked the door, saying, "The prince is waiting for you. Go now and see him!" When she reached the royal house, her stepsisters, who were already there, began to mock her. Hearing the commotion, the prince ordered her to approach.

Dressed in her rags, Haliya drew near, lovingly took the prince's hand and gently removed the ring. The prince was overjoyed and exclaimed, "You are the one! Today you shall be my bride!"

The wedding was a joyous occasion. Haliya wore a beautiful gown from the magic tree, and the Spirit of the Forest came as her special guest. Her father returned in time to witness her happiness. Meanwhile, the stepmother and stepsisters were banished to the chicken yard, where they remained for the rest of their days.

The prince and Haliya lived happily for many, many years, sharing their joy and wealth with all the people of the island.

RESOURCES

Original music and lyrics for "Mother Bathala's Song" by Debora Petschek.

The Gossamer Thread

KELLY MARIE BARHAM

THERE WAS ONCE A ROYAL COUPLE who lived in a castle made of stones and seashells, on an island out in the deep blue sea. They had beautiful gardens and fruit trees, and many good friends and neighbors, and the friendly fishermen always brought them a delicious daily catch. But they did not have a child, and of course they wished for one. Each night as the sky grew dark, they wished on the first star, and each morning at dawn, they prayed to the last morning star.

Finally one morning as they walked along the beach together, they spied a basket floating into shore, and in it they found a wee little baby sleeping peacefully, with eyes tight shut. As there was no boat in sight, they felt this must be the child of their prayers and wishes, and they vowed to give her the best of care, and to love her as their own.

They named the child Delia. She was a happy baby who brought them great joy. Though she grew into a healthy strong girl, she never opened her eyes, for she was blind. Because of this, her parents did not allow her to use sewing needles, scissors, matches, or any kind of tool, for they did not want her to hurt herself. She was never allowed to go outside alone, for they did not want her to go too near the ocean, or to trip and fall on the rocks. She longed to run free, and to work with her hands, but everyone in the castle insisted that she must be kept safe inside. She began to feel sadder and sadder until she was no longer happy at all.

Finally, the King decided to sail his ship to a faraway land to look for a doctor who could heal Delia's eyes, so that she could be happy and free. As he prepared for his journey, Delia begged him not to go, for even though she wished for sight, she loved the king so much she could not bear to be away from him. So the King asked the rope makers to weave a long rope, the longest rope in the world, out of the finest silk and wool, and they rolled it into a giant ball. The King placed the end of the rope in his daughter's hand, and the rest of the ball on his ship.

"Hold onto this rope until I return, and in this way we will always be connected," he said to her.

As he sailed away, Delia stood on the shore, holding tightly to her end of the rope.

A small hut was built for her on the shore, so that she could sit safely while she waited. She held tightly to the rope, and it stretched out many miles, until the ship itself was far out of sight. Many days and nights she sat, holding the rope as it pulled and went slack, and pulled and went slack. She knew her father was on the other end, and this gave her comfort.

However, as it happens on the big blue sea, one night a dark storm came rolling in. The winds blew fiercely, and tugged mightily on the rope. Finally, with a loud crack, the rope snapped out of Delia's hands and flew off into the sea. The girl was heartbroken. All of the people of the island feared the worst, that their Captain and King's ship was lost in the storm, along with the rope which connected them to each other.

The wise Queen said to Delia, "Perhaps, my child, you will never see with your eyes. But it is time now for you to learn to see with your fingers."

She took the sewing box out of the cabinet where it had been locked away, and began to teach the child how to make perfect stitches, by feeling them with her hands. Delia sewed for herself a sturdy apron, and always kept a pair of small scissors in her pocket.

"And," said the Queen, "it is time for you to learn to see with your ears, and even your nose."

They went into the garden, and Delia learned to smell the ripe fruit, and to name the birds by the songs she heard them singing. She learned to find the carrots that were ready for harvest by feeling the tops, and she learned to smell the rain before there was a cloud in the sky.

"And now," said her wise mother, "it is time for you to learn to see with your feet."

Together they climbed the cliffs, walked along the rocky shore, and even swam in the shallow tidal pools by the sea. Delia could see with many parts of herself, but she still wished to see the face of the King most of all.

One day, as she sat pulling weeds in the garden, she heard a fluttering, and a thump of something small falling to the ground nearby. It was a mourning dove, knocked to the ground by a hungry hawk. Delia picked it up. She could feel its heart still beating, and its broken wing. Carefully, she wrapped the dove in her apron, and gently carried it to her room in the castle tower. She wrapped the broken wing, and fed the dove fresh fruit and breadcrumbs, until it was healed and ready to fly again. Delia called the bird "My Little Heart," and they became such good companions that it did not want to leave without thanking Delia for saving its life.

"What can I do for you, dear friend, before I fly back to my nest?"

"Ah, My Little Heart," said Delia. "My only wish is to see the face of my dear King again, who is lost at sea, but there is nothing to be done about that."

"We shall see," said the dove, and she flew out the window.

Days went by, and Delia went about her work, imagining the little dove back with her own bird family. She smiled to think about it. But on the third day, as she was walking along the cliffs above the sea, she heard a familiar fluttering sound, and turned her face to the sky. It came closer and closer, until she felt the weight of the dove land on her shoulder, and its talons grasp tightly onto her skin. She reached up to touch the soft feathers, but instead of feathers she felt the soft end of the silk and woolen rope which the dove held in its beak. Delia began to weep with joy, and her mother and all of their attendants came running. They began to pull together on the rope, and slowly, slowly, more and more rope fed through their hands. It was hard work. They called the fishermen to help them, and soon all the people of the island were on the shore tugging together, rolling the rope into a big ball. They were pulling the ship back to harbor.

"Can you see it yet?" Delia kept asking, but for hours the answer was "No."

Finally, a great cheer went up from all the people, and Delia knew the ship would soon reach shore. It seemed only a moment before she heard the sound of her father's boots on the sand, running to scoop her into his arms. He held her tightly, and then, he also wept.

"My dearest," he said to Delia and the Queen, "our ship was lost in a mighty storm, we knew not where we were, nor how to get back home. I never found the healer nor the faraway land, and have returned with empty hands. If not for this little dove, we might never have found each other again." He was filled again with sorrow for his little blind daughter.

"But father," she said, "look. My wise mother has taught me to see with my fingers and I have sewn the apron. She has taught me to see with my ears, and I have made friends with the birds. I have learned to see with my feet, and even with my nose. And My Little Heart has brought you home again. I have everything I could wish for. Do not cry, my King."

The King was amazed at all the things she could do, and at how free and happy she was, just as he had always wished her to be. One last tear of joy rolled down his cheek as she turned her face up towards him, and it fell right into her own eyes. She blinked once, then twice, and exclaimed in surprise, "Father! Your eyes are the same color as the sky!"

And then, truly, she could see with her whole self, and the whole island celebrated. And if the night has not gotten too dark, they are there still in their castle of seastones and shells, only they have turned it into a lighthouse so that anyone who goes out to sea can find their way home again.

The Weaving of Karu and Resa

ANNIE SOMMERVILLE-HALL

ONCE THERE WAS A LITTLE GIRL who lived in a happy village with her family and friends. Her name was Resa. The village was on the bank of a wide river. The river flowed on and was rich with fish swimming and jumping and plants growing. On the sides of the banks grew long strands of thick grasses. The villagers wove these into baskets.

One morning Resa came down to cut grasses by herself for the first time. She had just become old enough to help with this task. The grass was thick and hard to cut. She was intent on her task. When she finally looked up, her eyes grew wide, as she saw another little girl from a neighboring village across the river. This girl was dark, dark as the purple-brown hills when the sun sets. Resa had spend most of her days near the heart of her own village, and had never seen anyone like the other little girl before.

The girl across the river was named Karu. Karu had never seen anyone as light as Resa, like the palest pink sky at sunset. Karu thought Resa looked too delicate to cut the grasses, and wondered what her name was. She smiled at her.

Resa was surprised to see such a smile of light.

They worked in silence, and when each girl started home they waved goodbye.

They came every day to the river at the same time. One day Karu brought Resa a pair of gloves she had made, just like hers, so that the grasses would not hurt her hands. Resa brought Karu a banana cake she had made. The girls swam toward each other to exchange gifts. Karu heard Resa laugh as she examined the gloves. "I did not know she would be so loud and curious," Karu thought. Karu took the bread, sniffed it, and smiled. "I did not know she would be so sweet and tender," Resa mused.

As they worked together on the riverbank, sometimes singing, laughing, or eating together, they began to get to know each other. Karu noticed that under Resa's skin she seemed to glow, almost a beautiful peachy color. Resa looked at Karu one day in the sun and noticed this same colorful glow in an exquisite brown. They became like sisters.

They asked their parents, aunts, and uncles to build a bridge over the river so that they could visit each other in any weather. The girls worked together, played together, and told stories together. They wove their baskets together out of many-colored grasses, and each basket had a story to tell. Sometimes in the evening they would sit on the riverbank together as the sun was setting and tell these stories as the villagers gathered around. Their stories were woven richly with color and friendship, just like their baskets.

And as they grew, they told stories to their children, and their children's children. They would all sit on the riverbank under a setting sun, listening to the sound of crickets, and the voices of these two sister friends, and look off into the rich dark hills, and the pale pink sky, and see the glow all around them.

Love Your Colors

NICKY MARTENS

THERE WAS ONCE A GROUP OF ELVES that lived deep within the forest. Now these were no ordinary elves—you see, they had been cursed. Once, long ago, they had tricked an old witch, and she was so cross with them, she turned them all invisible! This made the elves' work very tricky indeed as they would lose each other among all the leaves. They would holler and shout and call all about, but in the end, they would simply run into one another!

This went on for quite some time until one day, they all decided they would discover how to take the curse away. They packed up some berries and mushrooms, and then they had to decide which way to go. They talked among themselves for quite some time, until one little elf called out, "To the mountain top we should go! The wise old owl who lives there surely will be able to help us." So it was decided that the elves would journey to the top of the mountain.

They wandered by streams and climbed boulders tall. They had snacks on sun-warmed rocks, and not one of them fell off! As evening came, they saw a tall old gnarled tree standing alone, with the colors of the setting sun behind it.

This, they knew, was the home of the wise old owl. Cautiously, they came to stand right below its branches, and waited for the sky to darken so the owl would come out. Just as the stars started to twinkle above, out onto a branch stepped the owl.

Now of course the elves knew she couldn't see them, so they called out to her: "Please, wise old owl, hear our story and help us if you can!"

The owl listened as the elves told her of their curse and their troubles. When they had finished, she called down to them, "There is a way to take your curse away, but you will have to journey far, and find help along the way."

"We will do whatever it takes," the elves told her.

"Then," she said, "you must seek the end of a rainbow, and once you reach it you must find a way to get to the top. When you reach the top you can each slide down and your colors will come back to you."

"Thank you, oh thank you!" the elves cried out, and the owl, knowing her work was done, flew hooting off into the night.

The elves decided to rest the night beneath the tree and start the next day, searching for the end of a rainbow. They searched far and near, under stones and over mountain tops.

One day, after a big rainstorm, they saw a rainbow! It looked like it was coming from across the sea. They built a boat, and off they sailed over wave and crest, until they reached the other side of the sea. As they got off their boat, there it was, the end of the rainbow!

They tried climbing up, but with no luck. How, they wondered, would they ever get to the top?

Just then a group of butterflies fluttered by, and the elves called out to them. The butterflies stopped at a nearby bush of flowers and listened as the elves told their story. Now you see, since butterflies have so many beautiful colors, they felt sad for the elves, and decided to help them get their colors back.

One by one, the butterflies carried each elf up to the top of the rainbow. Once on top of the rainbow, the elves could not contain their excitement and down they went, each sliding down a different color, some sliding back and forth across all the colors of the rainbow! What fun this was, for you see a rainbow is one of the best slides there is.

When they reached the soft grass of the earth below, they all had a new color, each different and beautiful. The elf who slid down the red part of the rainbow was red, and the elves who slid down the orange and yellow parts were orange and yellow. Each elf became a different color of the rainbow. Some elves slid back and forth, and ended up being a beautiful blend of colors.

With their colors restored, the elves thanked the butterflies, and journeyed back home to the forest. To this day, these elves celebrate all of their different colors. Whenever they see a butterfly or a colorful rainbow, they are grateful, for now their colors are as beautiful as the wings of a butterfly!

Phoebe

NARGES MOSHIRI

This story was submitted by Lauren Hickman, who was Narges Moshiri's teacher in the early childhood education training. Narges wrote this story as a final assignment for the training in 2011. Narges passed away peacefully at her home in 2013. She was 54.

ONCE UPON A TIME, long long ago, there was a mother and her daughter, Phoebe, who lived in a small cottage by the woods. Though they were poor, they were happy and loved each other dearly. Each morning the mother would rise from her sleep and prepare sweet porridge for them to eat and all the while she would sing:

> *Phoebe in a rosebush*
> *Phoebe in a tree*
> *There's many a Phoebe in the world*
> *But you're the one for me.*

And after they finished their breakfast, Phoebe would help her mother with the housework. They worked all morning until the little cottage was neat and clean and shone like the golden sun. Then Mother would put a loaf of bread and a jug of water in a basket, which she had lined with a pretty white cloth. This she gave to Phoebe to take with her into the woods.

All day Phoebe would play in the woods and gather sweet berries for their supper. The animals who lived in the woods were not afraid of her, nor were the birds. The little hare would eat a leaf out of her hand, the deer ran merrily with her, and butterflies danced around her. And when she lay down to rest, the birds would sing their sweetest songs to her.

One winter's day the mother did not feel well, and so she stayed in bed. Phoebe went about doing the housework until the cottage was neat and clean, just as her mother had taught her.

Mother looked at Phoebe with kindness and knew that no harm would ever come her way. She called Phoebe to her side and told her that the time had come for Mother to return to the heavenly kingdom.

"Do not worry, my dear child," said Mother. "Though you may not see me, I will always watch over you. Listen for me in the sounds of the woods."

And with these last words, Phoebe's mother closed her eyes and died.

The kind people in the village helped Phoebe bury her mother under the poplar tree next to the cottage. And as she sat by her mother's grave, Phoebe sang:

> *Hundreds of stars in the pretty sky,*
> *Hundreds of shells on the shore together,*
> *Hundred of birds that go singing by,*
> *Hundreds of lambs in the sunny weather.*

> *Hundreds of dewdrops to greet the dawn,*
> *Hundreds of bees in the purple clover,*
> *Hundreds of butterflies on the lawn,*
> *But only one mother the wide world over.*

The days passed and Phoebe lived alone in the small cottage. Every morning after her breakfast of sweet porridge, Phoebe would busy herself with the housework until the cottage was neat and clean and shone like the golden sun. Then Phoebe would put a loaf of bread and a jug of water in a basket, which she had lined with a pretty white cloth, to take with her into the woods. All day Phoebe would play in the woods and gather sweet berries for her supper.

One spring day Phoebe was walking in the woods, her heart full of sadness. A tear rolled down her cheek and fell upon the ground. She bowed her head to look for it, and there on the ground she saw a small egg. She picked it up and said: "Dear little egg, all alone in the world."

And she wrapped it carefully in her kerchief and walked home.

Phoebe took great care of the egg and kept it warm, until one day she heard a crack, crack, cracking sound. She ran to her room, and there on the table a small bird had hatched from the egg.

Phoebe fed the bird for many days, until one day the bird's feathers had grown long enough for her to fly. Phoebe opened the cottage door. The bird flew out and settled on the poplar tree and sang: "Fee-bee, fee-bee, fee-bee!"

Phoebe lived a long long time ago, but you can still hear the phoebe bird calling her name: "Fee-bee, fee-bee, fee-bee!"

Phoebe in a rosebush
Phoebe in a tree
There's many a Phoebe in the world
But you're the one for me.

RESOURCES

Clyde Watson, "Phoebe in a Rose Bush," from Catch Me & Kiss Me & Say It Again *(New York: Philomel 1992).*

George Cooper, "Only One." See, e.g., Edmund Stedman, An American Anthology *(New York: Houghton, Mifflin and Co 1901) p. 1205.*

The Thrifty Tailor

A FOLKTALE ADAPTED BY DAN O'GARA

This story was submitted by Kathy Fraser, who learned it—one of her favorite all-purpose tales—from master story-teller Dan O'Gara, who was based in California's North Coast and passed away in 2013.

"The Thrifty Tailor" is ideal for audience participation because of the way repetition is used in the narrative, and also lends itself easily to the adoption of hand gestures that the audience can mimic.

Kathy sometimes tells the story while holding a large silk scarf, which she folds in half each time the story comes to the "worn-out" part.

ONCE, THERE WAS A VERY THRIFTY TAILOR. He created the most beautiful clothing for people, and he never threw out anything that might have a use.

He discovered one day, after making an outfit for someone, that there was enough fabric left over to make himself a cloak.

So he got out his scissors . . .

> *Gesture cutting with scissors*

. . . and he cut and he cut.

He got out his needle and thread . . .

> *Gesture sewing*

. . . and he sewed and sewed.

When he finished, he had a wonderful cloak! He liked it so much, and it fit him so well, that he wore it, and he wore it, and he wore it.

He wore it until it was . . .

If using a cloth during story-telling, fold cloth in half

all worn out.

BUT . . . he only thought it was worn out. When he looked again, he saw that there was enough fabric left over to make himself a large scarf.

So he got out his scissors . . .

Gesture cutting with scissors

. . . and he cut and he cut.

He got out his needle and thread . . .

Gesture sewing

. . . and he sewed and sewed.

When he finished, he had a handsome, large scarf! He liked it so much, and it fit him so well, that he wore it, and he wore it and he wore it.

He wore it until it was . . .

If using a cloth during story-telling, fold cloth in half again

all worn out.

BUT . . . he only thought it was worn out. When he looked again, he saw that there was enough fabric left over to make himself a very fine hat!

So he got out his scissors . . .

Gesture cutting with scissors

. . . and he cut and he cut.

He got out his needle and thread . . .

Gesture sewing

. . . and he sewed and sewed.

When he finished, he had a dapper little hat! He liked it so much, and it fit him so well, that he wore it, and he wore it and he wore it.

He wore it until it was . . .

If using a cloth during story-telling, fold cloth in half again

all worn out.

BUT . . . he only thought it was worn out. When he looked again, he saw that there was enough fabric left over to make himself a snappy bow tie!

So he got out his scissors . . .

Gesture cutting with scissors

. . . and he cut and he cut.

He got out his needle and thread . . .

Gesture sewing

. . . and he sewed and sewed.

When he finished, he had a charming bow tie! He liked it so much, and it fit him so well, that he wore it, and he wore it and he wore it.

He wore it until it was . . .

If using a cloth during story-telling, fold cloth in half again

all worn out.

BUT . . . he only thought it was worn out. When he looked again, he saw that there was enough fabric left over to make himself a cloth-covered button.

So he got out his scissors . . .

Gesture cutting with scissors

. . . and he cut and he cut.

He got out his needle and thread . . .

Gesture sewing

. . . and he sewed and sewed.

When he finished, he had a unique button, which he fastened to the top of his favorite coat! He liked it so much, and it fit him so well, that he wore it, and he wore it and he wore it.

He wore it until it was . . .

If using a cloth during story-telling, fold cloth in half again

all worn out.

BUT . . . he only thought it was worn out. When he looked again, he saw that there was enough fabric left over to make . . . a story.

And that is the story you've just heard!

About the Contributors

Louise deForest (Editor) was a Waldorf early childhood educator for many years and now consults, lectures, and teaches internationally. She is a WECAN Board Member and Regional Representative for Mexico, and one of two North American representatives on the council of the International Association for Steiner/Waldorf Early Childhood Education (IASWECE). She also edited *For the Children of the World: Stories and Recipes from IASWECE* and *Tell Me a Story: Stories from the Waldorf Early Childhood Association of North America*, both published by WECAN.

Deborah Grieder (Illustrator) graduated from Green Meadow Waldorf School in 2017, and is currently a junior at Muhlenberg College studying Neuroscience and Theatre. She spends her free time reading, drawing, painting, and indulging her newfound love of coffee with friends, preferably all at once! She is happy to have her illustrations included yet again in this new collection of wonderful stories.

Jo Valens (Illustrator) is a recently retired Waldorf early childhood teacher living in Great Barrington, Massachusetts. She co-illustrated the original *Tell Me a Story*, and is the illustrator of *The Waldorf Kindergarten Snack Book*, *The Waldorf School Book of Soups*, and *The Waldorf Book of Breads*.

∾

Candice Achenbach (*The Golden Cape of Courage*) has been a Waldorf early childhood teacher for twelve years. She wrote "The Golden Cape of Courage" for a child in her class who was having trouble finding the courage to leave his parents to come to school. She currently works with two private Waldorf families in the Pittsburgh area and is renovating a multi-family house from the 1880s with the hopes of offering housing, a supportive community, and child care to low-income families.

Anna Antonova (*The Snow Maiden*) was born in Moscow, Russia, and often went down to visit her grandmother on the family's ancestral farm. Her grandmother used to tell many stories passed down through an oral folklore tradition, in the dim light of the fireplace. After that, the woods around Anna's home seemed to gain a truly magical aura. She loved exploring them. After she grew up, Anna found that she didn't enjoy the jobs she took in engineering and computer technology, and quit both of them and to work with schools and arts and crafts, building towards becoming a Waldorf teacher. She now shares her passion and the wisdom of the folk tales with children.

Kelly Marie Barham (*A Place for a Baby to Sleep, Mrs. Mouse and the Maple Leaf, The Gossamer Thread*) works with the youngest students at Maine Waldorf School. Her lifelong love of magical story threads began on childhood Sunday afternoons, walking in the woods of North Carolina, building fairy houses, and listening in rapture to the stories her great aunt loved to tell. This led to her love of sharing natural and imaginative worlds with children through Waldorf education. Married to David Barham, Kelly is the proud mother of Jakeb, Eliza, and Adriel, who sometimes still listen to her tall tales, and now have a few of their own.

Carolyn S. Bailey (*The Legend of the Dipper*) was a prominent American children's author. Among her many publications were the collection *For the Children's Hour* and the Newbery Medal winner *Miss Hickory*.

Leslie Burchell-Fox (*The Child and Sister Star*) has been an early childhood educator for 24 years. She taught at the Waldorf School of Baltimore and is currently at the Green Meadow Waldorf School's Child's Garden at the Fellowship Community. She is also the Co-Director of the Waldorf Early Childhood Teacher Education program at Sunbridge Institute. She is passionate about building intergenerational intelligence in young children. One of her favorite artistic activities is Lazure painting; she also loves to dig in her garden.

Mary Caridi-Gorga (*Dragon Tears*) has been an early childhood educator at the Davis Waldorf School in Davis, California for nearly twenty years. She has enjoyed working with children, parents and colleagues in many capacities and especially loves singing, songwriting, dancing, walks, circle, and, occasionally, writing stories. She is the proud parent of a Waldorf graduate.

Patricia Carlin (*A Story for Finny and Theo*) is an early childhood teacher at the New Amsterdam School, a Waldorf school in New York City.

Aime Chevalier (*Rum-Ti-Pum-Pum*) assisted in Meg Fisher's nursery classroom at The Hartsbrook School in Hadley, Massachusetts. She created a puppet show based on a children's book she found in the library, and she made her own elephant puppet for it. With its subtle environmental message, "Rum-Ti-Pum-Pum" was a welcome addition to Mrs. Fisher's collection, and Aimee's lovely gray elephant remained with the other nursery puppets, delighting children for many more years.

Rebecca Davis (*Little Black Cat*) is the parent-child class teacher at the Waldorf School of Pittsburgh.

Toni de Gerez (*Louhi, Witch of North Farm*) was of Finnish descent and lived in Mexico. Beloved as an educator and founder of La Biblioteca Publica de San Miguel de Allende, she was also a poet and author of children's books.

Joanne Dennee (*Old Grandmother Pumpkin, Seed Babies*) feels blessed to be artfully collaborative with families, building the soil and soul of community via farm, food, and forest education for over forty-five years. Her greatest inspiration has come from wonder for the Earth herself, Native teachers, children and teaching Waldorf early childhood, Biodynamic training, and farmers—all of which continually deepen her commitment. The principle that the "Earth is Our Medicine" has guided her work at the Lake Champlain Waldorf School, New Village Farm, Poker Hill School, Food Works, Common Roots, the Qewar Social Project in Peru, and Sophia's Hearth.

Lucy DeWolf (*The Little, Small, Wee, Tiny Man*) was buoyed by wonderful teachers and supportive colleagues in the Early Childhood Education training at Sunbridge College. Her practical experience came through working as nursery assistant to Mary Beth Melton at The Waldorf School of Lexington. She has led nursery, mother and child classes, a home program and drop-in programs in Lexington, MA and briefly in Blue Hill, Maine. In retirement, she has many wonderful memories of the children.

Sacha Etzel (*Flame*) came to Waldorf education in 1989 after living in Mexico, the Polynesian islands, and Europe. She completed her Waldorf teacher training in 2000, while leading a Waldorf-inspired home program on a farm and also raising her beloved children. She volunteers for underserved communities, teaches mixed-aged kindergarten, family-child classes, student teachers, mentors and administrates—and loves writing!

Meg Fisher (*Little Spring Bunny, Mouse Gets Ready for Winter, Mr. and Mrs. Bird Build a Nest, Rum-Ti-Pum-Pum*) taught in the nursery program at The Hartsbrook School in Hadley, Massachsetts for seventeen years. "My favorite job ever!" She especially enjoyed circle and story time, and, as do all Waldorf early childhood teachers, she actively collected ideas for puppet shows, mostly relying on traditional stories and verses, but sometimes creating her own.

Peggy Finnegan (*The Winter Spiral*) lives in Anchorage, Alaska, where the winters are long and dark, and the return of the light at winter solstice is especially welcome. She taught at the Anchorage Waldorf School for six years and since then has been enjoying having a home kindergarten program. She wanted to create a story that gives a living picture of the winter spiral festival to the children, deepening our connection to the wonders of the living world around us.

Nancy Forer (*Little Duckling, Halloween Pumpkin Story, Twinkle*) delights in sharing stories, simple puppetry and songs with her young grandchildren. She was a founding/pioneering parent at the Waldorf School of Princeton (New Jersey) where she assisted in the nursery/kindergarten and taught a parent-child class. She now participates in a storytime program with Head Start in rural North Carolina.

Kathy Fraser (*The Pumpkin House, The Little Boy Who Had Adventures, The Thrifty Tailor*) grew up in a family rich with storytelling and loves to share stories for learning, laughing and healing. Kathy teaches at a tiny, independent school deep in the wooded mountains of northern California.

Mary Loomis Gaylord (*Seed Babies*) was an American teller of tales for children. Her stories have been published in many collections.

Carol Grieder-Brandenberger (*Chippy and His Family*) has over many years worked with women, infants, and children as a maternal-child health nurse. Before joining Green Meadow Waldorf School as a nursery teacher in 2006, she taught art classes and Parent & Child classes in a Waldorf-inspired nursery school in New Jersey. She is currently teaching in the Kindergarten.

Kayti Henry (*A Bridge of Hope*) has been a Waldorf teacher for thirteen years. She wrote "A Bridge of Hope" to help a child in her class whose parents were going through a rough divorce. She teaches at the Valley Waldorf City School in California.

Lauren Hickman (*Phoebe, Returning to the Heavenly Gardens*) has worked in Waldorf early childhood education for nearly thirty years, and is a passionate advocate for young children and parents. She has been a Waldorf school Administrator and is a former Executive Director and Early Childhood Department Chair at Rudolf Steiner College. She is a mentor, consultant, and evaluator for early childhood programs in both Waldorf and public schools. She teaches early childhood courses at American River College and is the Director of Pedagogy at the Davis Waldorf School. Her three children have all attended Waldorf schools from kindergarten through 12th grade.

Susan Howard (*How Glooskap Found the Summer*) is the Coordinator of WECAN and a member of the Coordinating Group of the International Association for Steiner/Waldorf Early Childhood Education. She is also the editor of a number of WECAN Books and the author of "The Essentials of Waldorf Early Childhood Education," most recently published in *Waldorf Early Childhood Education: An Introductory Reader* (WECAN 2017).

Silvia Jensen (*The Snail and the Butterfly*) is Brazilian. She has worked as a Waldorf early childhood educator at Anabá Waldorf School in Florianopolis, southern Brazil, for 26 years. She as a strong connection to storytelling and also likes to write stories.

Ruth Ker (*Nikolai, the Woodcarver*), a Waldorf school pioneer and an early childhood teacher for over 35 years, is now an Early Childhood Program Director for West Coast

Institute, a WECAN Board member and a travelling mentor for teachers and schools in North America. Ruth is also the author/editor of three books, *You're Not the Boss of Me* (2007), *From Kindergarten into the Grades* (2014), and *Please, Can We Play Games?* (2018), all published by the Waldorf Early Childhood Association of North America.

Mary Knighton (*The Lamp Lighter*) has been a Waldorf early childhood teacher for the past 25 years. She helped pioneer the Madrona School on Bainbridge Island, Washington, including its Nature Kindergarten. She is especially passionate about bringing nature experiences and developmental movements to young children.

Joanie Lackie-Callighan (*Mr. Snowman's Search, Little Boy Blue*) is happy to share her puppet stories with you. Recently retired, she'd spent many years teaching in public early elementary classrooms, then in a play-based preschool. She now spends her days hand-stitching toys to nurture the imagination. Visit her at her Etsy store, FairyTaleWonderShop.

Kate Lawes (*The Littlest Bear and the Leaf*) owns and operates Tree of Life Playschool, a home-based childcare in Victoria, British Columbia. She is a graduate of the West Coast Institute in Waldorf Early Childhood Education, is certified in early childhood education by the Pacific Rim Early Childhood Institute in British Columbia, and is certified as a Forest and Nature School Practitioner by the Child and Nature Alliance of Canada. Tree of Life is nature-based, with most days spent completely outside in local natural parks within Victoria's inner city. Kate also has a background in social services, theatre, and woodwork; loves singing, dancing, and backpacking; and has recently become an activist for climate awareness.

Connie Manson (*The Little Red Hen*) is a Waldorf early childhood educator and music teacher at Suncoast Waldorf School in Palm Harbor, Florida, and the founder and director of Starlite Puppets. Visit her at starlitepuppets.blogspot.com.

Mary Mansur (*A Flower To Be Found*) is a kindergarten teacher at the Waldorf school of Lexington in Massachusetts. She has been keeping bees for about 25 years, practices sustainable biodynamic beekeeping techniques, and is a graduate of the beekeeping program at Spikenard Farm.

Nicky Martens (*A Tool Story, Love Your Colors*) is an author and illustrator of therapeutic stories for children. Therapeutic stories use metaphor and journey to support children in their processing of a wide variety of experiences. As a Waldorf early childhood teacher, her love for the power and magic of stories has deepened. She believes these stories may be used to build connections and strengthen community. Nicole is also an illustrator, who creates works of art by using an array of mixed media including needle felting, fabric and natural materials.

Olive Beaupre Miller (*Wee Robin's Valentine Song*) was an American writer, publisher, and editor of children's literature.

Carlene Mogavero (*Juno and the Sun Maiden's Garden*) began her journey with Waldorf Education in 1994 as a parent in the initiative that has become The Waldorf School of DuPage, where she has been teaching kindergarten for thirteen years. She received her certification in Early Childhood Education at The West Coast Institute in Vancouver, British Columbia where the trees are magnificent and ancient and tell their own stories. She brings her love for the circle of seasonal festivals to life with her young students in movement, song, and story, also bringing her class to spend time among the trees of her own small woods every day.

Narges Moshiri (*Phoebe*) was born in Abadan, Iran, and came to the United States for university. A graduate of Boston University and Harvard Divinity School, she received certification in Waldorf early childhood education from Rudolf Steiner College. She taught at the Waldorf School of Louisville and founded the Cottage Garden Kindergarten. Narges crossed the threshold of death in 2013.

Mary Natale (*Mama's Bed*) has been in the Early Childhood Faculty at the Toronto Waldorf School for fifteen years. She's worked as the afternoon assistant and after care teacher in both the nursery and the kindergarten. Currently she teaches kindergarten. Before earning her certificate in Waldorf early childhood education, she taught kindergarten in Catholic schools for ten years.

Dan O'Gara (*The Thrifty Tailor*) was a master storyteller based in California's North Coast.

Sharifa Oppenheimer (*The Princess and the Dragon, Wee Robin's Valentine Song, A Story Sequence for Early Winter*) is the author of the best-selling book *Heaven on Earth: A Handbook for Parents of Young Children* and its companion workbook *How to Create the Star of your Family Culture*. Her newly released book, *With Stars in Their Eyes: Brain Science and Your Child's Journey Toward the Self* examines the traditional gentle ways of educating young children through art, poetry, song, movement, stories, creative play and immersion in the natural world. She was the founding teacher of the Charlottesville Waldorf School where she taught kindergarten for twenty-one years. She is the founder and former director of the Rose Garden, a home-based early childhood program. Sharifa's three grown sons were educated in the Waldorf tradition. She lives with her husband in an enchanted forest in Virginia.

Jan Patterson (*Sampo Brings Back the Sun*) is Director of Waldorf Early Childhood Teacher Education at the Rudolf Steiner Centre, Toronto, Canada.

Deborah Petschek (*The Sarimanok and the Secret Garden*) has had an avid interest in fairy tales since childhood, especially tales of many lands. She is a Waldorf early childhood educator in the kindergarten at the Seattle Waldorf School in Seattle, Washington.

Andrea Lee Pisacano (*Aloysius, the Keeper of Wishes*) was destined to be a teacher as the eldest of six children, with a pediatrician papa and an opera-singing mama. Andrea found her wings teaching after having three sons and moving to Kauai, Hawaii, where she was a class teacher and music teacher at the Kauai Waldorf School. She began a nursery at home after the birth of her fourth child and has been working with parents and children in Waldorf education for over 33 years. She loves writing stories, making puppets and painting.

Terri Rinehart (*The Fiercest Little Animal in the Forest*) is a retired Waldorf kindergarten teacher who lives in Western Massachusetts with her husband, Chris. She enjoys writing, knitting, gardening, and exploring the beautiful countryside near her home.

Diana Ross (*The Little, Small, Wee, Tiny Man*) was a teacher and storyteller who published her work in the 1940s-60s. Many of her stories were originally written for the BBC and were also broadcast in Australia, New Zealand, and Canada. She illustrated many of her fairy stories herself under the pseudonym "GRI." She had "a knowledge of what is needed in Nursery Schools . . . extremely useful to anyone in charge of children, whether one or two in a family, or twenty and thirty in a Day Nursery or School." (From www. diana-ross.co.uk/nursery)

Susan Silverio (*The Great Maple*) was the first teacher at the Ashwood Waldorf School initiative. When the school "grew up and moved out" to a more central location in Rockport, Maine, Susan continued Spindlewood Waldorf Kindergarten and LifeWays Center in Lincolnville, Maine, where the children participated in tapping the maple trees and collecting the sap in the late winter. Susan retired after 30 years of teaching in Lincolnville.

Annie Sommerville-Hall (*Auntie Lila's Garden, The Weaving of Karu and Resa*) has been a Waldorf early childhood teacher at the Waldorf School of Atlanta since 1993 in both the kindergarten and nursery. Each year with the parents and children in her class, she collaboratively sews a quilt on a theme, "following a thread" just like a story can! She enjoys weaving stories from her experience in the world around her, and from the growth and understanding that the children bring. She finds inspiration for a story when the muse presents itself in an interaction, a challenge, in witnessing nature and relationships—in life.

Stephen Spitalny (*The Bear, The Chief and His Two Daughters, Dragon Pearls*) is an early childhood consultant and writer, offering lectures, workshops and mentoring around the world. He is on the faculty of the Waldorf Institute of Southern California. He is the author of *Connecting With Young Children: Educating the Will* (2011), *Living with Young*

Children (2015), and *What's the Story: Storytelling as a Path Toward Living Happily Ever After* (2015). He has been a WECAN board member and editor of *Gateways* Newsletter.

Susan Starr (*Granny Evergreen and Her Gnome Helpers, Farmer Pete's Pumpkin Patch, The First Months of Life*) trained at Wynstones Waldorf Kindergarten Training in England with Margret Meyerkort, and was a Waldorf early childhood educator for 30 years. Since taking the Juniper Tree Puppetry Training with Suzanne Down from 2003-2005, she has enjoyed developing stories and putting them to puppetry. She is among many supporting Waldorf early childhood work in China. She now mentors the next generation of teachers, lecturing and leading workshops, and enjoys sailing San Diego Bay with friends.

Lise Stoessel (*The Giant and the Gnome's Gifts, The Hungry Dragon*) is an author, artist, and educator who has worked at the Charlottesville Waldorf School since 1990. She began in the nursery as an assistant to Sharifa Oppenheimer, who encouraged and inspired her to take up teaching as a lifelong path. Lise received her Masters Degree in Waldorf Early Childhood Education from Sunbridge College in 2006. She is delighted to offer these stories for others to enjoy for years to come.

Jenny Taylor (*The Rolling Pumpkin, The Silver Pine Cones, A Reverse Rainbow Bridge Story*) is a kindergarten teacher at the Mulberry Waldorf School, in Kingston, Ontario. In addition to teaching, Jenny has supported the governance of the school as the Early Childhood pedagogical chair and the Governance (full faculty) chair. Prior to joining Mulberry Waldorf School, Jenny taught in mainstream schools and completed a Ph.D. in Education at Queen's University. She is a parent of three Waldorf students.

Mindy Upton (*Minka and Twilight*) was, until recently, the Executive Director of Blue Sky Kindergarten in Boulder, Colorado, which she founded over 25 years ago. She is on the board at The National Institute for Play and has been an adjunct faculty member of Naropa University since 1980, where she teaches "Kindergarten Magic," a hands on course in the practice and application of early childhood pedagogy. Her quest is to nurture and embrace the magic of the early childhood years with love and attention to each individual child.

Diane Van Dommelen (*The Animals Visit Mother Earth, The Secret Prince, A Legend of the Pussywillows*) has been involved with Waldorf education since 1992. She began teaching at the Anchorage Waldorf School in 1994. Diane has also loved teaching handwork, mentoring, and homeschooling in the Waldorf tradition. She has been the grateful leader of the Pussy Willows, her Waldorf-inspired home pre-school, since 2017.

Andree Ward (*Little Apple Mouse, Grampsy's Apple Walk*) has been a kindergarten, nursery, and parent-child teacher at Hawthorne Valley Waldorf School in Ghent, New York since 1982, and currently teaches parent-child classes. She is a core member of the Alkion Center faculty were she directs the Early Childhood teacher training.

Wahsonti:io (*Sampo Brings Back the Sun*) is a graduate of the Waldorf early childhood teacher training, at Rudolf Steiner Centre Toronto. She is Mohawk, of the Six Nations of the Grand River Territory.

Wendy Weinrich (*Rosie's Adventure on the Icy Pond*) has been a Waldorf Kindergarten teacher since 1996, and completed her training at Sunbridge Institute. She also has completed the Nurturing The Roots program out of Denver, Colorado. She is founder and director of Mountaintop Waldorf School in Saugerties, New York. She is continually striving to expand her understanding of young children and their needs.

Jerre Whittlesey (*A Baby Is Coming*) was a kindergarten teacher at Live Oak Waldorf School for many years. While teaching kindergarten, she began the parent-child class, which birthed the program. When an illness made it impossible for Jerre to teach kindergarten, she transitioned into the parent-child program, and continued with that work for many years. She loved working with the early childhood, and "A Baby Is Coming" comes from her own need for a parent-child Advent story.

We were unable to locate any biographical information on Linda Grant (*Little Cloud*).

∼

About WECAN

The Waldorf Early Childhood Association of North America (WECAN) was founded in 1983, originally under the name of the Waldorf Kindergarten Association of North America.

WECAN's mission is to nurture a new cultural impulse for the work with the young child from pre-birth to age seven, based on an understanding of the healthy development of the child in body, soul and spirit, and on a commitment to protect and nurture childhood as the foundation for a truly human culture.

Membership in WECAN is open to early childhood programs, kindergartens, child care centers, home programs, and teacher training centers committed to the ideals and practices of Waldorf early childhood education, and to individuals who wish to support and contribute to Waldorf early childhood education in North America.

WECAN is a tax-exempt non-profit organization with an administrative office in Spring Valley, New York. WECAN works very closely in collaboration with its sister organization, the Association of Waldorf Schools of North America (AWSNA). WECAN is also a Full Member Association in the International Association for Steiner/ Waldorf Early Childhood Education (IASWECE), based in Järna, Sweden.

For a listing of WECAN member schools and programs,
information about becoming a Waldorf early childhood educator,
resources for living and working with young children,
a calendar of events in North America and worldwide,
and much more, please visit our website:

www.waldorfearlychildhood.org